William Senior, George Hildreth Goldsbrough

The old Wakefield Theatre

William Senior, George Hildreth Goldsbrough
The old Wakefield Theatre
ISBN/EAN: 9783743333611
Manufactured in Europe, USA, Canada, Australia, Japa
Cover: Foto ©Thomas Meinert / pixelio.de

Manufactured and distributed by brebook publishing software (www.brebook.com)

William Senior, George Hildreth Goldsbrough

The old Wakefield Theatre

CONTENTS

	PAGE
I. THE THEATRE	1
II. TATE WILKINSON	21
III. CONTRASTS	45
IV. THE PALMY DAYS	73
V. CONTINUATION AND DECADENCE	115

PREFACE.

This little book sufficiently explains its own origin and scope. I have here only to gratefully acknowledge my indebtedness to the many friends who have given me the benefit of their local knowledge; and especially to Dr. Wright, for MS. notes of playbills in his possession, and of his visits to the Theatre; to Mr. Percival Barratt, for the loan of books of theatrical history; to Mr. Charles Skidmore, Mr. G. V. Ellerton, Mr. Henry Clarkson, Mr. W. H. Hughes, and Mr. George Wright, for permitting me to see and take notes of playbills; to Mr. Fred Simpson, for the loan of plans; to Mr. George Roberts, of Lofthouse, for a note from Hewitt's papers; to Messrs. Sherwood and Banfield, for their courtesy in showing me over the building; and to the latter for information respecting its last years.

W. S.

Wakefield,
    October 15th, 1894.

I.

THE THEATRE

Here's a marvellous convenient place for our rehearsal,
—*Midsummer Night's Dream.*

IME was when plays taken from the Scriptures, and ranging in subject from the slaying of Abel to the tragic end of Judas, were wont to be presented in the fields hard by the parish church of Wakefield, and perhaps, earlier still, within the church itself. These primitive dramas, which may yet be read by persons of unusual perseverance, were native productions, written as well as acted in the neighbourhood; and their performance attracted so great a concourse of people to the town, as to originate, in the opinion of the local historian, the bestowal of the epithet "merry" upon it. Whether what

THE THEATRE

are now known as the Towneley Mysteries are in fact responsible for the—to us moderns—certainly somewhat mysterious juxtaposition of this adjective with the name of Wakefield may be left to the decision of the learned. That Wakefield, towards the end of the fifteenth century, was a dramatic centre seems indisputable: and it is a fact that one may perhaps be pardoned for alluding to in this place, slightly connected though it be with the subject of these notes—the modern Wakefield stage. If, instead of containing only notes, the following pages could boast of being a history, the introduction at the outset of the Wakefield Mystery Plays would no doubt be quite in accordance with the practice once, and perhaps yet, fashionable amongst topographers, of beginning as much as possible before the beginning. I possess a *History of Knaresborough* that opens in this impressive manner with an allusion to the colonists sent

THE THEATRE

out by the Greeks and Phœnicians. It hardly accounts for Knaresborough, but it shows, of course, a certain amount of research on the part of the historian. But as I cannot lay claim to the name, I have no right to appropriate the method. There is, however, in this case the excuse that the mystery plays of the later middle ages really were here — actually presented upon the very ground we of Wakefield tread; and, as it was in the form of plays for the playhouse that its crowning glory was added to English literature, for a town to have been associated even with the crude beginnings of our drama is surely something to be remembered. And it may be that the reminder of this ancient local connection will add a little pleasant antiquarian colouring to the love with which the present inhabitants of Wakefield (some of them) regard an art still exhibited in their midst—an art, indeed, as perennial as human nature itself.

THE THEATRE

The modern Wakefield stage—a stage in no wise central, nor differing from that of many another country town, and yet at one time a social institution of some importance—means, of course, the recently demolished playhouse in Westgate. Opened in September, 1776, the year in which Garrick closed his career, it stood for one hundred and eighteen years; no great length of life for ordinary bricks and mortar, at any rate as our forefathers used them, but rather remarkable in a theatre, the sort of place that usually has a Phœnix-like habit of rising from its own ashes at much shorter intervals. Escaping somehow this fate, the old Wakefield Theatre remained during the whole of that time one and the same building, and during the greater part of the period must be considered to have been the head-quarters in Wakefield of dramatic art, good, bad, or indifferent, as might happen to be dictated by the drama's patrons for the time being, in accordance with

THE THEATRE

the hackneyed line of Dr. Johnson's prologue. As such its annals reveal much that is interesting concerning the tastes and the manners of people, not, it is true, very remote from us in time, but still in some ways unlike us ; they illustrate the changes that have taken place in the old order of things theatrical, and they contain names, not a few, of more than provincial fame. The majesty of Mrs. Siddons, the vivacity of Mrs. Jordan, the classic grace of John Philip Kemble, and the passionate intensity of Edmund Kean have each been exhibited within its walls on more than one occasion ; and amongst performers of the second rank who have appeared upon its stage the names at least of O'Neill, Smithson, Vestris, Celeste, Charles Kemble, Emery, Charles Kean, Wallack, Phelps, and Bedford are still remembered. It is as no mere praiser of past times that I enumerate them ; there were giants in those days no doubt, but the all-round artistic merit of stage representations was, I am persuaded, never greater than it is to-day. But these names show that this curious old building had been included in the orbit of many 'stars,' and was once a provincial theatre as good as any. And, moreover, just so far as it seemed insufficient to us was it interesting as a record of what was considered sufficient in times past.

The house in Westgate was during its long existence the only regular theatre in the town— it used to announce itself on the bills simply as " Theatre, Wakefield,"—but other places have been occasionally used for dramatic entertainments, and some of them may be noted in passing. Before the theatre was opened there were two rooms, both apparently attached to inns, which were taken possession of from time to time by the strolling player; the one situated in the Bull Yard, and the other in the George Yard. These we shall meet with hereafter. The Assembly Room at the old White Hart, a

THE THEATRE

room said to have been about the size of the present Music Saloon—and in which, by the way, Stephen Kemble once gave recitations—was also during the early part of this century sometimes turned into a theatre. And in the York Hotel Yard, formerly Post Office Yard, is a warehouse, the upper floor of which was many years ago known as The Corn Market Theatre, the stage and gallery whereof still face each other in dusty silence. Here Incledon sang, between a melodrama and the farce. A single wooden stair leads up to what was the auditorium, and, except through the latter, the miniature stage was only reached by some stone steps outside the building. There have also been theatres, probably of the portable order, at various times in the Borough Market and in Wood Street; and of course the 'new' Corn Exchange was, and is, utilized for stage-plays. These, however, were but the more or less temporary camping-places of the Thespian waggon.

THE THEATRE

At the date of the erection of *the* Theatre (1775-6) the site was the property of one James Banks, in whose family it remained for upwards of sixty years afterwards. Many stories are told of the mild eccentricity of Mrs. Banks, who lived in the large house in Drury Lane, just behind the theatre, and who exercised, in virtue of her ownership, the privilege of giving a certain number of free passes to the boxes. This lady was Dr. Wright's patient for some months, about the year 1833 ; but, he says, his services were dispensed with because he could not approve of her diet of toasted cheese and tarts, "the only things she could eat." After her death, which under these circumstances is not, perhaps, to be wondered at, the heirs of James Banks, none of whom bore his name, conveyed the theatre on the 23rd January, 1839, to Joseph' Smedley, "then residing at Gainsboro', in the County of Lincoln, comedian," who had already been the manager for

THE THEATRE

some time. Smedley's widow sold it in 1865. By this time, so far as I have been able to discover, the reputation of the house had begun to wane. On the 30th June in this year Melinda Smedley, widow, and Georgiana Smedley, spinster, conveyed to one Nathan Webster, of Wakefield, comedian, "All that building lately used as a Theatre, but now as an Alhambra," by which, no doubt the lawyer who drew the deed meant a music hall. Such it had now become, and, forsaking the error of its earlier days, knew the dangerous dialogue of the dreadful stage-play no more for many years. Those ancient Greek ladies, the dramatic muses, if they had for a long time any further connection with it, were at most but its casual mistresses. They could hardly be expected to feel quite at home in a place which dubbed itself after a Moorish palace, and added the incongruity of a "beer on" license. Even Webster seems to have reformed, and dropping the comedian, to have

THE THEATRE

settled down into a simple beerhouse keeper, under which designation he sold the property in 1869. He no doubt derived this title from the fact of his having established just within the door of the theatre a drinking bar, through which the auditorium, now devoted to what somebody once called the least intellectual of the arts—meaning music, not drinking—could alone be reached. The theatre changed owners once or twice during the next year or two—perhaps it had become a rather speculative property; and in September, 1871, it was conveyed to John Brooke, who kept the Black Horse public-house close by, under the painfully precise description of "that building lately used as a Theatre, but now used as a Concert or Music Hall . . . part whereof is now used as a Beerhouse by the said John Brooke." It was now at the bottom. Without going into the actor-manager controversy, which concerns only 'the profession,' it is at all events best for

THE THEATRE

the playgoer that a theatre should be managed by an actor: and in its best days the Wakefield theatre always was. A well-intentioned attempt in 1883 to raise it, and to give Miss Melpomene and her sister exclusive possession, "as of their former estate," was only partly successful; and in November, 1892, the last stage-play was performed upon its boards.

The theatre remained standing until March, 1894, and its appearance both without and within is familiar to many. It made no pretension to architectural distinction. Except for its three principal doors, side by side, and the iron and glass canopy or awning over them—a modern excresence—its façade differed but slightly from that of the plain, square dwelling-houses of red brick, dating from the eighteenth century, which are still a striking feature of the street. One would rather have pictured the theatre as it stood in the spacious, residential Westgate of ninety

THE THEATRE

or a hundred years ago, amongst the mansions of its well-to-do patrons, and with pleasure-gardens within a stone's throw, than have shown it as in its latter days it was, sandwiched between the harmless, necessary, but unpoetical establishments of a pork butcher and a retailer of hot fried fish and chipped potatoes. That, however, must be left to the historical imagination of the reader. Its general outside resemblance to the neighbouring residences was increased by the roof, which was covered with brown slates, and sloped upwards from all four sides at the same angle as theirs; though against this must be placed the fact that chimneys were conspicuous by their absence. Above the three doors was a kind of arcade of three round-headed, shallow depressions in the wall, from the middle and largest of which looked out a square window; an architectural device of the period, ingeniously meant to give variety, of

THE THEATRE

which several examples are to be seen close at hand. Higher still, two circular and similarly purely ornamental depressions, like eyes, supported, in the heraldic sense of the word, the centre gallery window. The middle door was distinguished by a round head, with a sort of Doric pediment over it, a feature that the new iron awning to a great extent concealed; originally, I think, this was the only entrance. Formerly the theatre was approached by some stone steps projecting into the pavement; but these in the general removal of all obstacles to modern hurry had been improved away, and the doors consequently looked unduly tall. In a note found amongst the papers of the late John Hewitt, hairdresser and historian, it is stated that on the occasion of certain public rejoicings—probably those at the fall of Napoleon—the manager, "besides the illumination in each window, placed upon each iron rail of the palisading in the front a large lighted

THE THEATRE

candle, which had a very pleasing appearance." Both railings and steps remained until comparatively recently.

The auditorium, like the outside, was plain and rectangular, and was capable of accommodating about a thousand people. The floor of the pit was level, and the two tiers, very narrow at the sides and all but square at the corners, did not slope towards the stage after the manner of boxes and gallery in theatres of modern build, but were horizontal also. Bare rows of undivided benches were the boxes in the old days; and, indeed, the utmost pinnacle of luxury the so-called dress-circle at any time attained was represented by a few cane-bottomed chairs of the common pattern. Round each tier ran an open balustrade of oak, such as one sees on old-fashioned staircases, or round the galleries of edifices devoted to more solemn purposes. Latterly, however, the balusters on the box-tier had been covered on the outside

THE THEATRE

with wood or canvas, somewhat crudely decorated to look like the fronts of modern circles, so that the effect of this pleasing resemblance was partly lost. But for this attempt at gaiety, and the act drop, the aspect of the auditorium was not dangerously exhilarating. Many of the pillars supporting the galleries were also of oak, and, indeed, except where they might have been of late years strengthened with iron here and there, the internal fittings, galleries, partitions, and staircases were all of wood. There was no proscenium arch appertaining to the structure of the building; the wooden frame through which the stage-pictures were presented to the audience was hardly more substantial than the scenery; and but for this slight partition, auditorium and stage were one large undivided apartment. It must therefore be considered fortunate that the common fate of theatres never overtook this one, and that without accident it came at last to be pulled down, to make way for the better arranged and more elegant house that now stands upon its site.

The stage faced towards Westgate, and what may be called the accessory apartments were to the spectator's right, in a narrow building running parallel with the length of the theatre on its eastern side. Here was the room used by the patrons of the boxes for refreshment, and which originally ran back beyond the auditorium into the magical region known as 'behind.' Where it adjoined the wings there was a hole in the wall through which tradition says the thirsty actor received *his* refreshment whilst waiting for his cue. The stage end of this room was, however, in recent times partitioned off, and used as a green-room. Immediately beyond, on the same side of the stage, a wooden staircase led by two flights to a long, narrow chamber above, and gave access also to the 'flies.' This chamber, unceiled, with open beams revealing the slates of the roof, was

THE THEATRE

the ladies' dressing room. It rather suggested Hogarth's picture, *Strolling Actresses in a Barn*—with the strolling actresses left out, of course, for it was untenanted when I visited it. Another barn-like place on the ground floor, further back still, served the purpose of a tyring-house for the gentlemen of the company. It is also variously described in plans that I have seen as a brewhouse and a stable, having been at times used as such. In 1871, during the music hall period, the whole of the space usually occupied by the wings on the right side of the stage (spectator's left) was boxed off, and would have afforded further accommodation for performers; but as it was impossible for anyone to make entrance or exit 'right,' so long as that state of things continued, it could never have co-existed with the playing of stage-plays, and must have been done away with when the theatre reverted to its original purpose. From the 'stable' there was a door into Vaudeville

THE THEATRE

Yard (the nomenclature hereabouts is of the stage, stagey) through the eastern wall, a portion of which, unlike the rest of the building, was of stone, and evidently of considerable antiquity. It is supposed to have formed part of the ancient Westgate Bar, and it had been utilized as it stood by the builder of the theatre, just as the western wall of the latter has been left standing, and is now incorporated with the new structure. The stage entrance was through the archway leading out of Drury Lane, or Play House Yard, as it was formerly called, before a thoroughfare was made through old Mrs. Banks's large garden into the Back Lane.

Such were the more striking features of the theatre opened by Tate Wilkinson, actor, author, and manager, in 1776, the fashionable resort of the exclusive little Wakefield world in the Georgian era. Standing upon its empty stage in the present year, just before it was pulled down,

THE THEATRE

"like one who treads alone
Some banquet hall deserted,
Whose lights are fled, whose garlands dead,
And all but he departed,"

it would have been easy to moralize. There is always something that touches one about the interior of a building that has witnessed the ebb and flow of successive generations, and not the less because it may have been devoted to their amusement, whilst they fretted their hour upon the wider stage of the universal theatre. But, after all, the 'yesterday's roses' kind of sentiment seems rather thrown away upon a place the chinks and crannies of which were found to be filled with nut shells, and, in truth, its time was fully accomplished. The roses belonged at the very least to the day before yesterday, and their odour, I am told, had become strangely changed. Artists who had to pursue their vocation in the old house have in these degenerate days been known to complain of its accommodation: and it was owing to representations made from behind the curtain to that guardian of 'the profession,' the Actors' Association, that the building as a theatre received its quietus. But it is now no more, and *de mortuis nil nisi bonum*.

II.
TATE WILKINSON

What ! This gentleman will out-talk us all.—
Taming of the Shrew.

THE little volumes of the mercurial first manager of the Wakefield Theatre are naturally the chief source of information as to its earlier years. Tate Wilkinson was born in London on the 27th October, 1739. His father, the Reverend Dr. John Wilkinson, of the Savoy Chapel, suffered transportation for offences against the Marriage Acts when Tate was but seventeen. Thrown thus early upon his own resources, and with a strong bent towards the stage, he contrived, after being rebuffed by Rich, of Covent Garden, to win the good offices of Garrick by an exhibition of his talents for mimicry, and made his first appearance

TATE WILKINSON

at Drury Lane as a torch-bearer in the last act of *Romeo and Juliet* under that great actor's management. This was in 1757. Coming to man's estate he afterwards appeared "in almost every principal theatre in the three Kingdoms," as he tells us in his *Memoirs;* giving a long list of them, with the three London houses, the Dublin, Bath, and Edinburgh theatres at the top, and Wakefield at the bottom. In 1766 he invested his savings—some two thousand pounds—in the York Theatre, and settled down to the management of the York circuit,—a position he maintained with credit during the remainder of the century. He was acquainted with everyone of importance in the theatrical world of his day, and many afterwards famous performers received a part of their training in his company. As an actor he seems to have been rather a clever imitator than a performer of much originality or thoughtfulness. As a writer he modestly disclaims all pretension to style ; and, in fact, his Bohemianism not seldom kicks against the requirements of consecutive narrative, and occasionally even breaks through the rules of grammar. But his writings show no little observation of human nature—especially 'professional' human nature—and withal a just knowledge of the principles of the actor's art. These, of course, he could hardly help acquiring. Something of the general character of his books and that of their author will appear from the passages relating to Wakefield, which are quoted in this section.

It seems to have been by an accident that Tate Wilkinson first turned his attention hitherward. He had been accustomed to take his company to Beverley after York, but having given offence to the Mayor of the former place he was compelled to seek 'fresh woods and pastures new.' For mayors were mayors then ; and when, one night in 1771, his worship of Beverley, Colonel Appleton, arrived at the Hull

TATE WILKINSON

Theatre after the termination of the customary time for reserving seats (the end of the first act), and found those he had taken already occupied, he took himself off " swelling with dignity almost to bursting, and vowing vengeance on the Wilkinson," as his victim puts it; a vow which he was still angry enough two years later to fulfil, when Wilkinson with his company visited Beverley, by refusing them permission to perform, and keeping them idle for the three weeks that they remained there. But the poor player had in those days to put up with scant justice from 'the quality,' of whose manners we shall presently have another curious illustration at Wakefield itself.

Under the circumstances it was unlikely that Wilkinson would try Beverley again in the autumn of 1774.

"Colonel Appleton's treatment about that time having rendered Beverley to me a very disagreeable and doubtful situation, I luckily obtained Wakefield for the season of the year usually allotted to Beverley, which on the first trial answered so exceedingly well that I had a regular and commodious Theatre built there, which is frequently honoured with an audience of elegance, not to be seen in many of the larger towns of this Kingdom."

The Wandering Patentee, from which this and the following extracts are taken, was written at various times between 1790 and 1795, and covers a period going back to 1765. It seems desirable to explain this in view of the Wilkinsonian habit of changing, without warning, from reminiscences to statements of facts existing at the time of writing, and *vice versâ*.

"The neighbourhood of Wakefield is opulent, genteel, and numerous; and whenever they please to be unanimous and patronize the Theatre, a stranger, even from London, would be astonished at beholding the number of gentlemen's elegant carriages attending that Theatre, to convey their wealthy and spirited owners to their neighbouring villas; several of which may be termed palaces."

This sort of thing could not but be gratifying to a "genteel neighbourhood," whose patronage our author continued to solicit from time to time for some years after the publication of his book. He now jumps back to the year 1774—where he was—and before "that Theatre" was built.

"We had a shabby Theatre there, but better than the inhabitants of that town had ever been accustomed to. Decent theatres in the country were almost unknown thirty years ago. We had to oppose Mr. Whiteley that season. However, we not only obtained victory but defeated and routed the enemy."

The enemy so superabundantly overcome was in possession of a theatre in the George Yard, and included in its ranks the celebrated Miss Farren, afterwards Countess of Derby, who was playing the part of Columbine in "a new Pantomimical Entertainment" or after-piece called *Old Mother Red Cap*. The "shabby Theatre" in which Wilkinson's company appeared was in the Bull Yard—"the bad little Theatre in the Bull Yard" as he elsewhere calls it—and whither he came again in September,

1775, pending the opening of the "regular and commodious" one—the house that lasted to our time.

The account given in *The Wandering Patentee* of the first season must be here reproduced on account of the light it throws upon the manners of the age, and the example it affords of Wilkinson's curious style, although the extract is somewhat lengthy.

"Mrs. Mattocks made me a compliment of her performance at Wakefield, on Saturday, September 7th, 1776, which was the first night of performing in the new Theatre of that pleasant town and neighbourhood. The play was *The Beggar's Opera*, Macheath and Polly, Mr. and Mrs. Mattocks, with *The Musical Lady*, that character by Mrs. Mattocks."

The reader will remember Elia's description of Mrs. Mattocks—"sensiblest of viragos." She was long at Covent Garden, retiring in 1807, but she lived until 1826.

"The race-week followed, and the new Theatre was greatly attended. Mr. Earle, of Beningbrough, near

TATE WILKINSON

York, was steward, and on a visit at Sir John Smyth's, near Wakefield. *The Hypocrite* and *The Author* was (*sic*) acted on Saturday, September 14. Every part of the evening's entertainment went off with such eclat as occasioned that truly well-bred gentleman, his lady and party, to stand up, bow, courtesy, &c., by way of approbation for their good entertainment. I was so puffed up with conceit and vanity, that I looked on myself as firmly seated in the opinion of box, pit, and gallery of my new theatre—but after sunshine comes a storm.

On Sunday, the 15th of September, I gave a dinner at the Black Bull, to some friends and the whole company. The banquet was good and plentiful. Success to the Theatre, and the healths of the worthy inhabitants of Wakefield, were drank in large libations, and nothing cross happened between the cup and the lip, though the cup and the lip frequently encountered each other; but each repetition was in a friendly, not a hostile manner. It grew towards night, yet all was well—neither scandal nor bickerings, either with the manager, players, or individuals disturbed our social board, nor did any hostile invasion interrupt our mutual felicity; and I felt as grand, and breathed as high as the flattered Alexander the Great at his banquet (which, by-the-bye, was the play appointed for the Monday night following) when lo! in all our calm, an unexpected storm arose, which had nearly set my famed Persepolis on fire; the particulars of which unfortunate circumstance were precisely as follow:"

TATE WILKINSON

But instead of giving them our manager shoots off into 'another story,' as Rudyard Kipling would say, returning to Wakefield, after a page or so, in this manner—

"On a Sunday night, September 15, 1776, as I have lately mentioned, a gentleman in liquor happened to be in the bar of the Bull Inn, which was the time of my public dinner, when Mr. Murray (a gentleman of family and an excellent actor, now at Bath), happened to be there; and I suppose from some wrong, or slight offence before given—as I would hope that no gentleman, unprovoked, could behave in so unbecoming a manner—the *gentleman* ordered the waiter to turn the *player* out of the bar; this produced a quarrel, and I dare say both were wrong, and warm with the juice of the grape when they proceeded to blows. The Monday night, after the play, some gentlemen acquainted with the *aggressor*, not only came themselves, but sent for some gentlemen thirty miles distant, to banish the manager, and shut up the theatre, for an offence that had been committed at the tavern—Good God! what is it a player had not better be, if such acts of power were often put in practice! Had Mr. Murray given any offence in his profession on the stage, that certainly was the place to decide, and to acquit or condemn. But if quarrels in taverns, or in private, are to be brought against the player at the theatre (allowing the player ever so culpable), it undoubtedly is an overbearing act, void of sense, reason, and every considerate good quality. I was called on for Mr. Murray to instantly come on the stage, and ask public pardon for having affronted a gentleman. Mr. Murray would not come when he was called, for he looked upon himself, he said, as the injured person; and as to asking pardon, he certainly never would do so, and thereby degrade himself. I was then called upon to dismiss Mr. Murray immediately. That I declared (and with truth) was not in my power, as Mr. Murray was under article to me, with a severe penalty attending the breach of that article; but that unless the gentlemen could settle the business to their satisfaction, Mr. Murray should not appear on the stage at Wakefield again. The riot lasted from nine o'clock to near one, as those gentlemen would not suffer the farce to go on."

The matter did not end there, for Wilkinson and Murray were sent for by "Mr. Justice Zouch" to the White Hart, where, says our manager—

"Every method was used to win or compel Murray to ask pardon, which he had the spirit to refuse. The House of Correction was then genteelly mentioned for me as well as the rest, as infringing on the Act of Parliament. Justice Zouch observed, that as Patentee of York, I certainly could not be committed as a vagrant, having a settled habitation; and he hoped Mr. Murray would think better of it."

Mr. Murray, however, did not think better of it, and the Wakefield public saw him no more. The theatre was boycotted for the rest of the season by the clique to which his assailant belonged, which, judging from the remark Wilkinson makes as to friendly relations between "the races and the company" not being restored for two years afterwards, seems to have been a clique not unconnected with that institution. This and the Beverley episode show that the path of the theatrical manager in the eighteenth century was not free from difficulty— except in stepping out of the frying-pan into the fire. Fortunately a lady came to the rescue.

"Lady Armytage sent her compliments for me to drink tea at Sir John Smyth's, that week of confusion. She seemed truly affected at the unlucky circumstance, particularly as the matter originated from a cause wherein the theatre had not any concern. Her ladyship bespoke a play on the Friday, September 20th, 1776, which occasioned a genteel and quiet audience. Indeed, the inhabitants one and all were violent in their wishes for the theatre, and in their attachment to Mr. Murray; and had it not been for that body shewing a determination to preserve the playhouse and actors from injury, I do not think it would have ended so well as it did. But here is a lesson that we should never be secure of happiness from appearances."

And so, pointing a moral, our manager records the closing of the theatre "in quiet," on Sept. 21st, and goes on to Doncaster.

The following season (1777) seems to have been only remarkable for the appearance of a Mr. Vincent as Romeo, on September 10th; a gentleman, we are informed, too lazy to make himself letter-perfect in his parts. He afterwards took orders, married money, settled in the neighbourhood, and condemned the stage from the pulpit; a course the last item of which Wilkinson naturally considers unhandsome under the circumstances.

The season of 1778 was so successful that Wilkinson was persuaded to return for an additional week later in the autumn, "the Company being greatly reinforced with Mr. John Kemble, Mr. and Mrs. King, Mr. and Mrs. Hitchcock, Mr. Wood (from the Haymarket), and a Mr. Waylett." He opened with Rowe's *Tamerlane*, with the following caste :—

Tamerlane ..	.. Mr. CUMMINS.
Bajazet ..	.. Mr. WILKINSON.
Selima ..	.. Mrs. INCHBALD.
Arpasia ..	.. Mrs. KING.

and *The Deserter*—

Henry ..	.. Mr. WOOD.
Simpkin ..	.. Mr. SUETT.
Louisa ..	.. Mrs. HITCHCOCK.

Cummins was a provincial favourite who remained in the York Company till his death in 1817, on the stage of the Leeds Theatre. Elizabeth Inchbald was afterwards well known as the authoress of two novels and a large number of plays. She would at

TATE WILKINSON

this time be considerably under thirty. Richard Suett, from 1780 to 1804 a member of the Drury Lane Company, was in those days famous for his representations of bibulous parts, the characteristics of which in later years he unfortunately studied far too introspectively. Kemble appeared on the Wednesday as Captain Plume in Farquhar's comedy of *The Recruiting Officer*. The future manager of Drury Lane and Covent Garden would be then only twenty-one. But notwithstanding this company of clever people the return visit did not justify Wilkinson's expectations.

On September 6th, 1779, the theatre was opened with "the altered play of *The Comedy of Errors*" and *The Apprentice;* but half an hour after the curtain should have been drawn up there was but the sum of thirty shillings in the house. This beggarly account of empty boxes Wilkinson explains by saying that it was before the races, and that the Wakefield people

TATE WILKINSON

"never, unless on some very extraordinary occasion, have hitherto attended the theatre before the race week, and then like a jack wound up to its height they find the way, and spin and flutter to the theatre, till its close for the season drops the weight." This, as he elsewhere quaintly puts it, was because "Everybody knows that Everybody will be there in that week, and that Everybody must be there when all the world is to be there." Wakefield, at this time, was nothing if not fashionable.

For the next five or six years the theatre was regularly opened in September, but the seasons appear to have been uneventful. The afterwards famous Mrs. Jordan, whose laugh, Hazlitt said, did one good to hear it, joined Wilkinson's company about 1782, and played in it at Wakefield as in other towns upon the circuit. In 1783 she played here William in the opera of *Rosina*—what Wilkinson calls "a breeches character"—and in 1785 was in receipt of £1 11s. 6d. a week. However, on September 9th of the last-named year she made, at Wakefield, her last appearance as a regular member of his company, and betook herself to London for 'betterment.' Her success was remarkably rapid, and the next year she was in a position to make her own terms with Wilkinson, namely, "shares"; indeed he, whilst acknowledging the lady's histrionic talents, and "her humanity and goodness to her late parent," is compelled, he says, "as Mr. Manager, to declare, like Mr. Foote in his 'Devil upon Two Sticks,' that Mrs. Jordan in making a bargain is too many for the cunningest devil of us all." As an actress, as everyone knows, she excelled in hoydens, as girls who ought to have been boys, and in the kind of part now called 'principal boys,' who are always girls. She continued on the stage until 1814, and died at St. Cloud, near Paris, two years later. One hardly goes to an epitaph for a faithful portrait, but that composed for Mrs. Jordan epitomises so well her strong points, and the tongue of Horace is in modern times so usually reserved for the praises of lives moulded on somewhat more conventional lines than hers, that I have ventured to copy it in a note.*

The year 1786 is memorable in Wakefield theatrical history for the first appearance of Mrs. Siddons. That great actress, at the mention of whose name Sir Joshua's stately portrait and almost statelier compliment inevitably come to mind, was then over thirty years of age, and no novice in her profession. Ten

* "M. S. Dorotheæ Jordan, quæ per multos annos Londini, inque aliis Britanniæ urbibus, Scenam egregie ornavit ; Lepore comico, Vocis suavitate, Puellarum hilarium, Alteriusque sexûs, Moribus, habitu, imitandis, Nulli secunda ; Ad exercendam eam, Qua tam feliciter, Versata est artem, Ut res egenorum, Adversas sublevaret, Nemo Promptior. E vita exiit Tertio Nonas Julii, 1816, Annos Nata 50. Mementote. Lugete."

years before, in the year in which our theatre was opened, she had made her unsuccessful *début* at Drury Lane, somewhat overawed, it would seem, by the reputation of Garrick, with whom she acted, and who was then just about to retire. From Easter to Whitsuntide, 1777, she was at York with her friend, our manager, playing, amongst other parts, Euphrasia to his Evander in *The Grecian Daughter*, and in 1782 had returned to the London boards, this time to conquer. Wilkinson—with whom she was on intimate terms, and whose daughter Patty continued her companion up to her last years—brought her to Leeds in September, 1786, and had evidently no intention at first of introducing the tragedienne to a Wakefield audience, she being under an engagement to go on to Liverpool almost immediately; but the Wakefield playgoers inserted in the Leeds newspaper a sarcastic acknowledgment of Mr. Wilkinson's "disinterested though unmerited attention to

TATE WILKINSON

them," and, as the result, Mrs. Siddons played Belvidera in *Venice Preserved* in Wakefield Theatre on the 6th September. The same week, on the Saturday, Mrs. Jordan played in *The Country Girl* and *The Romp* two of her best impersonations; but Wilkinson observes that "Melpomene's bowl and dagger having left such an awful gloom, even Thalia could not laugh, or if she did it was very mortifying, as it was to herself almost without company, or any throng of visitors." The receipts on the Wednesday when Melpomene played (at London prices) were £67 6s. 6d. *The Romp* only produced £38 12s. This also was before the race-week. Stars, be it observed, had to be brought to attract the Wakefield people into the theatre before their wonted time; during the carnival (of horseflesh) when they went to stare at one another the stock company sufficed.

Among the plays given at Wakefield during

TATE WILKINSON

the season of 1787 were Bickerstaff's *Love in a Village, Lionel and Clarissa,* Bickerstaff's *Padlock, The Duenna* (a comic opera by R. B. Sheridan), *Comus,* Bickerstaff's *Maid of the Mill, The Beggar's Opera,* and *The Deserter.* Kemble appeared again the following year, 1788, playing Othello, Richard III., and Hamlet, on September 3rd, 4th, and 6th. In June, 1789, his greater sister came again, this time for two nights, playing Jane Shore and Isabella, and Wilkinson opened as usual in September. Lady Pilkington gave her patronage one night, and Wilkinson acted Cadwallader in Foote's Play of *The Author,* by desire of Lady Mexborough. He finished the season September 21st with Shylock.

Nothing of importance is recorded of the season of 1790. On September 5th, 1791, was performed (for the author's benefit) a comedy called *The Lucky Escape,* written by Mr. Richard Linnecar, of Wakefield, and the next year, on

TATE WILKINSON

September 19th, this gentleman had another benefit, when his five-act tragedy, *The Generous Moor* was produced. These plays, together with another comedy entitled *The Plotting Wives*, sundry songs, bacchanalian, patriotic, and descriptive of the charms of Chloe, some 'Strictures on Freemasonry,' and verses 'On the Death of a favourite Pug, wantonly Killed by a Stone,' had been printed in 1789; the volume is still extant and well deserves the title of *The Miscellaneous Works* of its author. Anyone, therefore, who obtains it may (possibly) read the five acts of very blank verse of which *The Generous Moor* consists; and though he will see at once why Mustapha, the bold, bad Dey of Tangier, after being stabbed by a fair but virtuous captive, and exclaiming "O I am killed!" should continue to do most of the talking through two subsequent scenes (the lady having been a little too hasty for the dramatist), he will probably have more difficulty in deciding whether Hasan, who turns Christian and commits suicide rather than survive his friend (who doesn't die), or Hali, who surrenders a dusky maiden (who won't look at him) to her Spanish lover is meant to be the more generous Moor of the two. "The receipt," says Wilkinson, speaking of the night when this piece held the Wakefield stage, "was the greatest I had ever known, being equal, at the common prices, to Mrs. Siddon's acting there at London prices." Who shall say that the masterpieces of dramatic literature are meant for the study after this?

Amongst the other plays performed at Wakefield during the season of 1792 were *The Provoked Husband*, by Vanburgh and Cibber (September 5th), and *The Gamester*, by Moore (September 7th). The theatre was closed September 24th.

Linnecar had another benefit in the autumn of 1793, but what was performed on that occasion I have not discovered. Perhaps it was the

TATE WILKINSON

remaining play of his trilogy, *The Plotting Wives*, which had been given at York in 1769; when, as he tells us, "It was not damn'd, but the Author was in Purgatory all the Time of its Performance," a remark, on the whole, funnier than anything in the comedy itself. This year seems to have seen the last of the Wakefield Races, the race-course coming under the provisions of the local Inclosure Act; and we find Wilkinson lamenting their abolition in the words of Shylock—"You take away my life when you take my means to live." Yet he says of the following year, "Wakefield season was full as good as I ever remember it;" and probably his estimate of the dependence of the theatre upon the races was an exaggerated one. No doubt during race-weeks and Assize-weeks the country towns were full of people from a distance on pleasure or business bent; but still there were the inhabitants, "violent in their wishes for the theatre," as he himself says, and they must have counted for something.

Amongst the other well-known actors of this time must be mentioned Elliston, of whom there is a full length portrait as Hamlet in the possession of Mr. Clarkson, of Alverthorpe Hall, and who was a member of Wilkinson's company for a year or two towards the close of the century. I do not know whether he afterwards visited Wakefield.

It appears from a letter written by Mrs. Siddons in May, 1796, that she was about to visit York and Leeds again during the summer of that year. Her next tour in the provinces was in the summer of 1801, and she may have appeared at Wakefield then. But we no longer have Tate's gossipy chronicle to help us to complete our peep at the Wakefield Theatre in the eighteenth century; which, by the way, he just outlived, dying in 1803.

III.

CONTRASTS.

How chances it they travel? Their residence, both in reputation and profit, were better both ways.—
Hamlet.

BEFORE following the fortunes of the Wakefield Theatre during the early part of this century, some points of contrast between the circumstances of a theatrical company at that time, and the touring life of to-day may be noted. For many of these the railway is, of course, responsible. Instead of being whirled by special trains from Hull to Brighton, and from Brighton back to Glasgow within the fortnight, the old managers made a consecutive and comparatively dignified progress through the single district in which their 'circuit' was. After York, Wakefield; after Wakefield,

CONTRASTS

Doncaster; sometimes a week at Pontefract, or an excursion to Sheffield; then to Hull "for winter quarters"; then York again (to take Wilkinson's usual round) and so on, every year. As a consequence, companies not only remained for several weeks in one place, but re-visited the same towns at stated intervals; and their members, often for some years substantially the same, became well known in their own proper persons to the public whom they lived to please. There was, indeed, a lower grade of much despised strollers, not attached to the regular theatres, but performing in inns, booths, barns, or wherever they could find a room, such as the band of "Jemmy Whiteley," whom Wilkinson found entrenched in the George Yard in 1774. And, on the other hand, there were the 'stars' and London people, whose appearances at country theatres for one, two, or three nights only, kept them at a celestial distance from their provincial admirers.

CONTRASTS

But between the two came the local stock companies, in whose leading performers the playgoing public took a pride as belonging to and reflecting credit on the neighbourhood. There was, for example, Wilkinson, for upwards of thirty years constantly at the head of theatrical affairs in Yorkshire; he speaks of his friends "in my own circuit." Then there was Frodsham, called 'the York Garrick,' considered doubtless by many of the inhabitants of that city the equal, and by himself certainly the superior of his prototype; and Cummins, who was so great a favourite that the gallery at York candidly informed Kemble himself that "he cudna shoot oot laik Coomens." Such men, and others, the London stage never tempted from the scene where their popularity was established. Cummins, it will be remembered, was acting at Wakefield in the seventies, and he continued a member of the York company until his sudden death on the Leeds stage in June,

CONTRASTS

1817, as he was playing in *Jane Shore*. No doubt in his later years he got to rant, to "shout out," to split the ears of the groundlings ; but he was regarded with a certain local pride. Witness the following from the columns of the Wakefield paper shortly after his death. The italics are mine.

"To his (the manager's) highly laudable design of appropriating the benefit of the first night to the benefit of Miss Cummins we would more particularly call the attention of our readers. The design, we understand, is to purchase an annuity for the oldest daughter of that once meritorious member of the histrionic corps. But a short time ago we had the sorrowful task of recording the awful and sudden affecting death of this worthy man while engaged in the discharge of his professional duties. Too well and too long have his merits as an actor been known to stand in need of any panegyric we can bestow. From youth to age have his talents been unsparingly exerted for the gratification of his auditors *within the sphere of this county*, where we may say succeeding generations have bestowed upon him their welcome applause. But not less were his deserts in the domestic circle, where he discharged with fidelity the sacred duties of husband, father, and of friend. These considerations,

CONTRASTS

we trust, will be sufficient to procure a full and overflowing assemblage on that occasion as a tribute of respect to departed worth, as a mark of the high admiration in which his talents and virtues were held, and of sympathy at the awful manner in which their exertion *here* was terminated."

This is interesting, besides, as a specimen of the journalese of the period.

And in those days the age of patronage had not yet passed away. The tradition of the Statute of Elizabeth inflicting penalties on "common players of interludes and Minstrels wandering abroad, other than players of interludes belonging to any Baron of this realm or any honourable personage of greater degree," seems not to have been extinct; and partly, perhaps, from force of ancient habit, as well as from considerations not unconnected with the treasury, the children of Thespis still sheltered themselves under the wings of the great ones even of small places. In the old days, as Mr. William Archer says, and as we have learnt from

CONTRASTS

our friend Tate Wilkinson, the strolling manager "had to be obsequious to the County, submissive to the Garrison, conciliatory to the Civic powers;" and for many years after this period of mere toleration had gone by, he found it desirable to invoke the special patronage of such "honourable personages" as the would-be fashionable would readily follow to his house. It was still, and long continued, customary for the manager to wait upon the influential people of the town and neighbourhood, and to invite them to select from the company's repertory such plays as they desired to be performed. In announcing the commencement of the season in 1822, the manager of the Wakefield Theatre, after regretting "that the lateness of the York August Meeting should abridge his continuance in Wakefield to One Fortnight," states that "he has not less than Forty Dramas, never performed here, to select from, so as to give Novelty to each Night." The "never performed here" must usually be taken *cum grano*; indeed, Wilkinson relates an instance of a play being advertised, not in the capital of Ireland, as " not played here these five years, for the second time this season." But the forty dramas is no exaggeration, and in the extensive repertories of the old stock companies, and the advantages they offered as schools for actors (proof whereof will be found below), we have another contrast to the present nearly universal system, under which a young artist—not necessarily idle or unambitious—may have to play but a single part for months that sometimes grow into years. The piece, then, having been chosen, the patron or patrons attended on the night with their friends and following, and each of the former was furnished with a bill of the play printed on white satin—the quaint, old-fashioned play-bill, which, again, whether its big capitals were impressed on satin or paper, was a different thing from the advertisement-covered programme of these days. From a number of Wakefield play-bills I have extracted the following examples of 'distinguished patronage' as interesting, and sometimes amusing by reason of the endeavour to make the play fit the patron.

"By desire of Lieut. Col. Tottenham and the Officers of the Royal Wakefield Volunteers, Their Majesties' Servants will perform the Comedy of *John Bull, or an Englishman's Fireside*" (this was in 1804, when Napoleon was expected). "By Desire of the Gentlemen forming the Committee of the Wakefield Dispensary" (1823). "Under the Patronage of the Members of the Gentlemen's Book Club" (1827). "By Desire, and under the immediate Patronage of the Ladies Patronesses and Gentlemen Stewards of the late Fancy Ball, the Play of *The Stranger*, if not otherwise commanded" (1828). "By Desire, and under the Patronage of the Stewards of the Assembly" (1836).

CONTRASTS

"By Desire, and under the Patronage of the Bachelors of Wakefield, Mrs. Inchbald's Comedy of *To Marry or Not to Marry*, with an Interlude called *Popping the Question*, and concluding with the Farce of *A Handsome Husband*" (1836). "By Desire, and under the Patronage of the Worshipful the Master, Officers, and Brethren of the Lodge of Unanimity of Free and Accepted Masons, *Secrets Worth Knowing*" (1837). "Under the Patronage of the Ancient Order of Foresters, *As you like it*" (1840). "Under the Patronage of the Gentlemen of the Wakefield Regatta Club, *The Mutiny at the Nore*" (1851). The following announcement, dated October, 1823, in which month the theatre was first lighted with gas, is sufficiently curious to be given here at length :—

"By Desire of the Gentlemen of the Wakefield Gas Light Committee, this present Friday, Oct, 31st, will be revived Reynold's Comedy of
HOW TO GROW RICH.

CONTRASTS

> After which a Serious Ballet of Action, written by
> Mr. Frimbley, entitled
> THE FIRE KING.
> At the end of the Ballet Mr. Bywater will sing Jolly
> Dick the Gas Light Man.
> The whole to conclude with a new Farce (never
> performed here) called
> CENT PER CENT,
> Or, Money Laid Out to Advantage."

If on this occasion Commerce patronized Art, the latter evidently did her best to advertise Commerce in return. In order that the repertory of the company might contain no less than three pieces so well fitted to the inauguration of the gas-meter I suppose the manager of 1823 must have been an adept at the minor art of 'writing up.' This system of patronage, which Kean disliked so much, has now nearly died out; and people go to the theatre to see the acting, not because so-and-so has bespoken a play.

It would appear that the relations between the playhouse and the public of provincial

towns were formerly somewhat more intimate—
perhaps personal would be a better word—than
is now the case. It entered more into the life
of the place. In November, 1827, the Wakefield paper announces that 'Mr. Calvert, of the
Theatre,' will explain the principles of elocution
in a course of five lectures: the first being
delivered, by permission of the magistrates, in
the Court House — a place where even now
such an explanation would not be always super-
fluous; and in December, 1836, on the occasion
of a benefit taken by a Miss Desborough (of
whom more hereafter), it is advertised that "A
Plan of the Theatre will be at Miss Desborough's
Lodgings, at Miss Watkins's, Wood Street,
where all Persons desirous of securing Places
are requested to apply." The old custom for the
actors to sell the tickets for their own benefits
was undignified, but it shows the personal
character of their popularity in small places.
Nowadays the 'benefit' is almost as extinct as

the 'bespeak.' But these friendly relations long continued, as is shown by the following advertisement, the first sentence of which unfortunately suffices to date it as belonging to comparatively modern times :—

"THEATRE ROYAL, WAKEFIELD.

An unknown Speculator, who had undertaken the management of the Theatre, having absconded with the proceeds of the first week's business, the Season is abruptly closed, and a number of Performers thus thrown suddenly out of Engagements. Several parties sympathising with the Company under such circumstances, and desirous of showing their kind feeling professionally,

TWO FAREWELL PIECES

have been arranged, and will take place on Saturday and Monday Evenings, February 17th and 19th, 1855, on which occasions the Dramatic Amateurs of Wakefield, in conjunction with the remaining members of the establishment, will appear, and solicit, the support and patronage of their friends."

Do amateurs now ever come to the rescue of the stranded?

Amongst the other differences between the earlier days of the Wakefield Theatre and the

CONTRASTS

present time must be mentioned the hour at which the performance commenced. It is well known that our hours have been gradually getting later. In Pepys's time plays began at three o'clock, but for the greater part of the eighteenth century six o'clock was the usual time for drawing up the curtain. Towards the end of that century the hour advanced. In a mutilated playbill of Wilkinson's Company (probably at Wakefield Theatre) in "an Entertainment in three parts, called *The Death of Captain Cook*," the time of commencement is half-past six. There is no date, but Captain Cook was killed in 1779, and we might safely assume that this representation took place within a few years afterwards, even if Wilkinson's name and the typography did not pretty well settle the question. In a Portsmouth playbill of 1791, printed in *The Wandering Patentee*, the performance begins "precisely at half-past six o'clock, on account of the variety of entertainments"; which seems to imply that half-past six was then earlier than usual. In 1804, at Wakefield, the performance began at a quarter to seven, and in 1805 at seven; and this hour seems to have long continued the customary one. Even in London, in 1851, *The Green Bushes* at the Adelphi began at seven o'clock; and in the same year the curtain at Wakefield was advertised to rise at the same hour. Exceptional occasions, of which we have records, only prove the rule. On the 9th April, 1828, "on this occasion, by desire of many, who purpose visiting (*i.e.*, the Wakefield Theatre) in Fancy Dresses previous to the opening of the Ball, the Performance will not commence till eight o'clock." The following evening, by the way, so enamoured do the 'many' seem to have become of themselves in fancy dresses, that the benefit of an actor named Bellamy was postponed in order that they might go again, "for the benefit of the Dispensary and House

CONTRASTS

of Recovery." And on New Year's Day, 1846, when *The Idiot Witness*, followed by a Christmas Pantomime, was in the bill, the manager considerately announced that "in order that the Younger Branches may have an opportunity of witnessing the New Grand Pantomime without the necessity of their being kept from their rest to too late an hour, the performance will begin at 6.30 and terminate between nine and ten o'clock. Seven was, however, the usual time. Now-a-days, a glance 'under the clock' reveals much later hours. Out of nineteen London theatres open on the same night in May last, two began at 7.40 and one at 7.45. These are the earliest. Six began at eight, six between eight and half-past, and four at 8.30; and at six of them the *pièce de résistance* does not begin until 8.50 or nine o'clock. The present provincial hours are no doubt earlier, but they tend in the same direction.

Of course, there was a good deal more

included in an average evening's entertainment in the old days than now; for with the earlier beginning I find no evidence of an earlier ending, and there seems no doubt that the playgoer of the first half of the century generally got very fair value, in point of quantity, for his money. The manager in 1847 informs "the Nobility, Gentry, and other Inhabitants of Wakefield and its Vicinity" that "the Performances on all occasions will be brought to a conclusion as shortly as possible after eleven o'clock," as if it would be reassuring to early people kept from visiting the theatre by the fear of even later hours. A good four hours' entertainment seems to have been the rule; as for to-day, I have more than one recent playbill in my possession whereon "Carriages at eleven" figures at the end of a programme that is not announced to commence until 8.30. A modern three-act play, taking but a little over two hours in actual representation, sometimes suffices for

CONTRASTS

the whole bill. Of the variety — not to say incongruity — of the items comprised in the old-fashioned programme examples will be found below.

The prices of admission to the Wakefield Theatre were originally: Boxes, 3s.; Pit, 2s.; and Gallery, 1s. We find them so stated in 1804 and in 1836. Boxes and Pit on special occasions were raised to 4s. and 2s. 6d. respectively, and in 1814 the management increased the ordinary prices to these figures. The Pit was reduced to 2s. in 1817. During the seasons of 1822-3-4-5 and 6 the prices continued at 4s., 2s., and 1s., and these were still the ordinary prices in 1831. By 1846 the Gallery had become a sixpenny one, and in the fifties we find a greater variety of the better seats: 'Dress Boxes,' 2s. 6d. (sometimes 3s.); 'Side Boxes,' 1s. 6d.; and 'Stage Boxes,' 2s. 6d. The Pit was by that time only 1s., and the Gallery still sixpence. These prices were much the same as those with which Mr. Sherwood opened in 1883, but which could not be maintained. The highest charges made for admission to the theatre of which I have found a record were those in October, 1821, on the occasion of a Concert: Boxes, 7s.; Pit, 5s.; Gallery, 2s, 6d. But the course of the regular theatrical prices, which alone here concern us, may be gathered from the notes given above. Sometimes season tickets were issued, enabling playgoers to visit the theatre at any time during the season for a lump sum. These are advertised in the forties, and again in 1860, and, of course, are a part of the old stock company system of continuing many weeks in one place and changing the play every night, which obtained until the present one-play-one-town-a-week tour became the rule.

The Wakefield Theatre during the eighteenth century and up to 1823 regularly opened its doors towards the end of August or beginning of September for about three weeks. In the

CONTRASTS

last-named year it was not announced to open until October 20th, and the season for some years thereafter runs into November. After the races were done away with there does not appear to have been any reason, other than old usage, for keeping to this time of the year, and we find the theatre sometimes open also in the Spring—for three weeks in February, 1814, for instance, and during part of March, April, and May in 1828. In May and June, 1821, it was open for eight nights, the performances taking place every succeeding Thursday and Saturday "till the whole shall be completed." That it was not unusual to close for one or two nights a week is shown by the announcement in the Wakefield paper in August, 1806, "A Play every night next week," and that on September 2nd, 1814, "On account of the shortness of the season the Theatre will be opened every evening." In 1833-4 the season extends from November 18th to January 21st, and the theatre opened again

CONTRASTS

February 4th to 29th, 1834; in 1836-7, from November 4th to January 6th, the Company only playing four nights a week. I have set out a list of the plays given during this season as showing the kind of dramatic fare provided for Wakefield playgoers more than half a century ago, and also the amount of work the old companies got through, and their value as training schools of dramatic art. As their decay is often justly lamented on this last ground, it may be interesting to revert for a moment to the Wakefield seasons of 1824 and 1825, when W. J. Hammond, afterwards a leading low comedian with Macready's Covent Garden Company, was serving his apprenticeship here. Between October 25th and November 13th, 1824, Hammond sustained no fewer than 20 different characters at Wakefield, and in 1825, during a season of similar duration, 15 new ones, besides giving comic songs between the pieces. They were but small parts, some of them, though in the

CONTRASTS

previous year, when he first appeared at Wakefield, he had played Acres, Trinculo, and Sir Andrew Aguecheek; but opportunities for gaining experience and discovering his true *métier* were thus afforded to the young actor which are not now so easily obtained.

PLAYS PERFORMED AT WAKEFIELD THEATRE DURING
THE SEASON OF 1836-7.

1836. *Followed by*
Fri., Nov. 4 The Rivals .. Three Pair of Lovers.
Sat., ,, 5 The Gipsy Chief.. The Young Widow, and Captain Stevens.
Mon., ,, 7 The Iron Chest .. Two Strings to your Bow.
Wed., ,, 9 The Deformed .. Turn out.
Fri., ,, 11 The Dream at Sea The Invincibles.
Sat., ,, 12 Venice Preserved. Past Ten o'clock and a Rainy Night.
Mon., ,, 14 The Deformed .. The Spoiled Child.
Wed., ,, 16 The Brigand .. Is he Jealous? and The Miller's Maid.
Fri., ,, 18 The Stranger .. The Invincibles.
Sat., ,, 19 Henry IV. .. The Dunder Family.
Mon., ,, 21 Hamlet .. .. A Dead Shot,
Wed., ,, 23 The Dream at Sea Love and Laugh.
Fri., ,, 25 King John .. High Life Below Stairs.

CONTRASTS

				Followed by
Sat.,	,,	26	The Way to Get Married }	The Vampire.
Mon.,	,,	28	My Poll and My Partner Joe .. }	Blue Devils, and The Captain is not a Miss.
Wed.,	,,	30	My Poll and My Partner Joe }	Hunting a Turtle, and The Irish Tutor.
Fri.,	Dec.	2	Ion ..	.. Too Late for Dinner.
Sat.,	,,	3	Luke the Labourer	The Invincibles, and The Unfinished Gentleman.
Mon.,	,,	5	(Dinner of Conservative Association. No Performance.)	
Tues.,	,,	6	The Belle's Stratagem }	The Happiest Day in My Life.
Thurs.,	,,	8	Richard III.	.. The Honest Thieves.
Fri.,	,,	9	Ivanhoe ..	.. Catching an Heiress.
Sat.,	,,	10	The Wandering Boys }	The Innkeeper's Wife, and The Mutiny at the Nore.
Mon.,	,,	12	Othello ..	.. Where shall I Dine?
Tues.,	,,	13	Speed the Plough	The Dumb Man of the Rocks.
Thurs.,	,,	15	Eugene Aram	.. The Wreck Ashore.
Sat.,	,,	17	Virginius	.. Hunting a Turtle.
Mon.,	,,	19	The School for Scandal }	The Widow's Victim.
Wed.,	,,	21	The Jewess	.. The Young Widow, and Nicholas Flam.

CONTRASTS
Followed by

Fri.,	,,	23	The Jewess ..	Simpson & Co.
Sat.,	,,	24	(Christmas Eve.	No Performance.)
Mon.,	,,	26	To Marry or Not to Marry }	Popping the Question, and A Handsome Husband.
Wed.,	,,	28	The Italian Wife..	The Married Rake, and Black Eyed Susan.
Thurs.,	,,	29	Eugene Aram ..	A Dead Shot.
Sat.,	,,	31	George Barnwell..	The Dead Alive.

1837.

Mon., Jan.	2	Secrets Worth Knowing }	My Uncle John.
Wed., ,,	4	The Idiot Witness,	Turning the Tables, and The Heart of a Soldier.
Thurs., ,,	5	The School for Grown Children }	The Illustrious Stranger
Fri., ,, (Last Night)	6	The Provoked Husband }	Three Fingered Jack.

The above list contains only the strictly dramatic part of the nightly programme, but it must be remembered that between the pieces was sandwiched a variety entertainment. For instance, after '*Luke the Labourer, or the Lost Son*,' two ladies appear in " the celebrated La Sylphide, as danced by Madem. Taglioni," and Mr. Compton gives "The Humours of an Election." The farce of *The Invincibles* follows, after which Mr. Compton sings another comic song and the two ladies again dance, before the second farce of *The Unfinished Gentleman.* After *Virginius*, on December 17, and before the farce, comes an overture by Mozart, Miss Desborough sings "Buy a Broom" in character, Mr. Hunt executes "a grotesque Chinese dance,' and besides comic songs there is a violin solo "*à la* Paganini" by Mr. Bywater. Strange as these combinations seem to us, the naive addition to the announcement in September, 1820, of *Macbeth* and *Coriolanus*—" In the course of the evening a Variety of Performances will be exhibited on the Slack Wire, Tight Rope, Flying Rope, &c."—is even more foreign to our ideas of artistic propriety. Such entertainments are now relegated to the 'halls,' but the modern music hall only arose, I think, with the London Canterbury in the late fifties.

CONTRASTS

Out of the regular season the theatre was used for occasional entertainments other than dramatic. That it was sometimes unoccupied for a considerable period may perhaps be inferred, not only from the absence of advertisements in the newspaper, but from such quaint announcements as that in January, 1812, "Care will be taken that the Theatre be well aired;" "The Theatre will be perfectly warm and accommodating by a powerful Stove," (in January, 1817); and "Good Fires will be kept in the House Several Successive Days" (February, 1823). A few instances of the non-theatrical nights may be given. On November, 15th, 1805,

"The Public are respectfully informed that the Entertainments which gained such universal Approbation on Wednesday last will be again repeated this Evening. Particularly a Variety of curious and interesting Hydraulic Experiments, and Mr. Saxoni's celebrated Performance on the Tight Rope. To conclude with Artificial Fireworks."

There is plenty of variety here, and one

cannot altogether repress a certain curiosity as to the artificial fireworks. In September, 1810, is exhibited in the theatre a

"Dioastrodoxon, or Grand Transparent Orrery, with all the *splendid Scenery* explanatory of the *Seasons, Eclipses, Tides, and Comets*, as exhibited in *London* and the *University of Oxford*. The whole forming the most *perspicuous* and comprehensive View of the WORKS of the CREATOR in the United Kingdom."

This must have been improving, and the show is advertised again in subsequent years; probably it was a provincial tour of the "Orrery Lecturer at the Haymarket" mentioned by Charles Lamb. Ventriloquists, Wizards, and Phrenological demonstrators appear from time to time; and on the 11th April, 1827, W. J. Hammond, the actor already referred to, gave a lecture in the theatre on "Peculiarities, Characters, Manners, and Sketches of Life, entitled, Trifles Light as Air."

Curious expedients were sometimes resorted to in order to attract people to the house even

CONTRASTS

during the regular theatrical seasons. On September 7, 1820,

"The Entertainments will commence at Seven o'clock with the Ascension and Descension of a Grand and Magnificent Balloon, designed, painted, and splendidly decorated in exact Imitation of the One which took its Aerial Excursion from the Thuileries (*sic*) in Paris in honour of the ever memorable Victory of Waterloo; during its Ascension and Descension from the back of the stage to the Gallery, the young American will perpendicularly exhibit himself on his Head!! Keeping Equilibrium during the whole of this unprecedented Feat of Agile Exertion. Immediately after will be performed the favourite Comedy called *A Roland for an Oliver*.

Upon an evening in April, 1828, the balloon plays a leading part in an unholy proceeding akin to a raffle, which is thus elaborately announced:—

"Great Novelty! A fine Pig to be given away! Each person on going into the house will be presented with a ticket on which a number is inscribed. This ticket is to be preserved until the conclusion of the first piece. A Balloon will then ascend containing

CONTRASTS

corresponding numbers to those given to the company, upon which they (*sic*) will fall upon the stage, one of the audience will then be selected, who, being blindfolded, will pick out a number, which being proclaimed, the holder of the same number will be entitled to the Pig!"

Amusing as I think some of these notices are, it is time to get back to matters more closely connected with the drama. A few of the more striking changes since the theatre was built I have tried to illustrate; others appear incidentally, but not less plainly, from what follows.

IV.
THE PALMY DAYS.

Time hath, my lord, a wallet at his back
Wherein he puts alms for Oblivion.
Troilus and Cressida.

IT may be interesting, in resuming the chronicles of the Wakefield theatre from the time of Tate Wilkinson's death, to mention the names of some of the plays popular at the beginning of the nineteenth century. In 1804 we find, August 31st, *Venice Preserved*, Jaffier, Mr. Meggett; Belvidera, Miss Fitzgerald; with *Love Laughs at Locksmiths*, Lydia, Miss Mills. September 1st, *The Soldier's Daughter*, written by Mr. Cherry. September 3rd, *Othello*, Mr. Meggett in the name-part; Roderigo, Mr. Melvin; Emilia, Miss Smith; with *Raising the Wind*, Diddler, Mr. Melvin;

THE PALMY DAYS

Sam, Mr. Knight. September 7th, *Macbeth*, with the Musical Farce of *The Paragraph*. September 8th, *The Mountaineers*, with the Pantomime of *The Fairy*. September 10th, *The Wife of Two Husbands*, with *Love Laughs at Locksmiths*. The Company then went to Pontefract for a week. September 17th, *John Bull*, Tom Shuffleton, Mr. Melvin; Dan, Mr. Knight; Lady Caroline, Miss Smith; with *The Jew and the Doctor*, Abednego, Melvin; Old Bromley, Knight; Emily, Miss Smith. September 20th, *The Will for the Deed;* with *The Highland Reel*.

In 1805, September 2nd, *Who wants a Guinea?* with *Raising the Wind*. September 6th, *Who wants a Guinea?* with the Pantomime of *La Perouse, or the Desolate Island*. September 7th, *The Wonder, or a Woman Keeps a Secret*. September 9th, *The Honeymoon*. The Company again went to Pontefract, returning to Wakefield on the 16th for a further

THE PALMY DAYS

week, during which *The School of Reform* and *The Shawl* were performed.

In 1806, August 29th, *George Barnwell*, with *Of Age To-Morrow;* September 30th, *The School for Friends*, with *The Hunter of the Alps;* September 5th, *Romeo and Juliet*, with *The Weathercock;* September 8th, *The School for Scandal*, with the Pantomime of *Provocation, or Spanish Ingratitude;* September 15th, *The English Fleet* (Trafalgar had been won the previous October), with *The Young Quaker*.

As I do not in these pages emulate, even on a small scale, the Reverend John Genest, whose History of the English Stage, in ten volumes, is a wonderful piece of industrious compilation, I shall not attempt to set out all the material which can be obtained towards an exhaustive list of the plays given in the Wakefield Theatre, or of the people who played in them. For a good many seasons

THE PALMY DAYS

this material exists; but a note of the visits of stars, and an occasional selection from the repertories of the stock companies, as showing the rise of new plays and the continuance of old ones in the public favour, will probably be sufficient for all but the theatrical antiquary.

In the season of 1807 Mr. and Mrs. Charles Kemble came to Wakefield for three nights. The plays were (September 2nd) *The Wonder*, Don Felix and Violante by the Kembles; and *The Prize, or 2, 5, 3, 8*, Caroline by Mrs. C. Kemble. On September 3rd they played Lovemore and the Widow Belmour in Murphy's Comedy of *The Way to Keep Him*, which was followed by *The Weathercock*, Variella (with songs), Mrs. C. Kemble; and on September 4th was given Kemble's play, *The Point of Honour*, in which he and his wife were cast for Durimel and Bertha; after which Mrs. C. Kemble and Mr. Wrench apeared in *Personation, or Fairly Taken In ;* the evening

THE PALMY DAYS

concluding with *High Life Below Stairs*, Lovel and Mrs. Kitty, Mr. and Mrs. C. Kemble. The bill states this to have been Charles Kemble's first appearance here; he made his first recorded appearance on any stage at Sheffield, not very far away, in 1792, being then but a boy, and in April, 1794, had appeared at Drury Lane. He excelled in old comedy parts. Wrench was an actor of considerable reputation, and was introduced to the London theatre-goers at the Lyceum in October, 1809, in *The West Indian.*

In the same year at Wakefield (August 10th), Mr. Incledon, of the Theatre Royal, Covent Garden, appeared, and a week or two later Mr. Emery was playing here for three nights in *The School of Reform, The Poor Gentleman*, and *The Miser.* Emery was great in Yorkshire parts, such as Tyke, and is also remembered for his Caliban, and his Silence in Henry IV.

In August, 1811, Mrs. Jordan revisited the

THE PALMY DAYS

scene of her novitiate for four nights, appearing in *The Pannell, A Trip to Scarborough, All in the Wrong,* and *Man and Wife.* Incledon appeared again in January, 1812, combining his talents with those of the elder Mathews, in an entertainment, then very popular, consisting of anecdotes and songs. In May next year, Mr. Doran had the theatre, and one evening in that month *Henry IV.* was played for his benefit. In February, 1814, Mr. Stanton took the theatre for three weeks, and announced the engagement of Mr. Betty, "his first appearance at Wakefield these seven years." William Henry West Betty, the quondam Infant Roscius, was the hero of one of the most extraordinary crazes in theatrical annals. Ten years earlier, a boy of thirteen or thereabouts, he had been the idol of London, a 'star' before whom for the moment even the Siddons and John Kemble had to give way. But the furore did not last long; by 1807 his attraction waned in London, though he was still

THE PALMY DAYS

much run after in the provinces. It would appear from the above announcement that he had visited Wakefield about the last named year. In the summer of 1808, being no longer young enough for an infant phenomenon, he had retired, and entered Cambridge University, but he returned to the stage in 1812. In his maturer years he seems to have been only a moderately good actor. During this Wakefield season of 1814 he appeared as Barbarossa, Sir Edward Mortimer in *The Iron Chest*, Pizarro, Alexander the Great, Hamlet, and as Tristram Fickle in 'the entertainment' of *The Weathercock*. He lived until 1874, having finally quitted the stage fifty years before.

Amongst the other plays performed this season were *The Soldier's Daughter, The Brazen Bust, Education, Who's to have her? The Miller and his Men, Lovers' Quarrels, Macbeth*, and the Burletta of *Tom Thumb*.

The Theatre was opened again, September

THE PALMY DAYS

2nd to 25th, 1814, during which season were given, amongst other pieces, *Every one has his Fault*, *The Wandering Boys*, *Blue Devils*, Macklin's *Man of the World* (Sir Pertinax Macsycophant, Mr. Fitzgerald; Egerton, Mr. Mansel), *Raising the Wind*, *The Jew*, *The Irishman in London*, *The School for Wives*, *Ways and Means*, *Henry V.*, *The West Indian*, and *The Honeymoon*. This was Fitzgerald's first season as manager.

The 1815 season opened on August 28th, when *The Poor Gentleman*, with the Musical Entertainment of *Rosina*, was given 'for the benefit of the Doorkeepers.' On August 29th, *The West Indian*, with *No Song no Supper;* September 1st, *The Forest of Bondy, or the Dog of Montargis*, with the original performing dog, "Dragon"; after which, *Blue Devils*, followed by a comic song, " *The Duke of Wellington the Dandy O!* " and concluding with the farce of *The Liar*. September 2nd, *The Cure for the*

THE PALMY DAYS

Heart Ache, with Sheridan's Comedy of *The Critic, or a Tragedy Rehearsed;* September 4th, *George Barnwell*, with *The Woodman's Hut;* September 8th, *The Foundling of the Forest*, with *Inkle and Yarico;* September 11th, *Richard III*, with *Of Age To-morrow;* September 14th, *Romeo and Juliet*, Miss Norton, of Covent Garden, as Juliet; September 15th, *The Child of the Desert*, with *Past Ten o'clock and a Rainy Night;* September 16th, *The Renegade*, with the Musical Entertainment, *Brother and Sister;* September 18th, *Wild Oats*, with *The Forest of Bondy;* September 19th, *As you like it;* and September 22nd, *Policy, or Thus Runs the World away, Intrigue*, and *Brother and Sister*. This was the last night, and Fitzgerald thus addressed the audience from the stage :—

" Ladies and Gentlemen, Impressed with the most lively sentiments of gratitude, I appear before you to offer my acknowledgments for the handsome manner in which the Theatre has been supported throughout the season. A report has been industriously circulated that, being displeased with the reception I met with, it was my intention to discontinue my visits to this town. I beg leave publicly to contradict the assertion, and to state to the inhabitants of Wakefield and its vicinity that if they are satisfied with my humble endeavours to contribute to their amusement I am perfectly contented with the encouragement I have received from them. I will not take up your time, Ladies and Gentlemen, by repeating those professions which experience only can prove to be sincere, but, for myself, and those by whom I have the honour to be supported, assure you that we look forward with an anxious pleasure to the period when we shall again have the honour to appear before you, and with the best wishes for your health and prosperity, most respectfully bid you farewell."

'Anxious pleasure' is good. Incledon appeared at the Theatre again on the 22nd March, 1816, in a miscellaneous performance, and the usual season followed in the autumn, when Fitzgerald acted *Tamerlane* for his benefit, and amongst the other plays given were *The Rivals*, *School for Scandal*, *The Man of the World*, and *George Barnwell*. The following year, 1817, Mr. Harley, of Drury Lane, appeared for six nights, commencing August 27, on which date was acted, for the benefit of Miss Cummins, already mentioned, Colman's *Poor Gentleman*, with the farce of *Love, Law, and Physic*. *The Honeymoon*, *The Wonder*, *John Bull*, *The Belle's Stratagem*, and *Guy Mannering* were also presented. I give below a copy of the play-bill on the benefit night of "Quicksilver" Harley, as he was called—

BENEFIT OF Mr. HARLEY,
And the LAST NIGHT of his Appearance.

Theatre, Wakefield.

On Thursday Evening, Sept. 4th, 1817,
Their Majesties' Servants will act a New Comedy, in Four Acts (never performed here), called
The Touchstone.

Paragon..........Mr. HARLEY.
(As originally performed by him at the Theatre Royal, Drury Lane).

Finesse ...... Mr. YOUNG | Countryman..Mr. PARSONS
Garnish......Mr. CARTER | Messenger .... Mr. WOOD
Circuit ...... Mr. HUMBY | Mrs. Fairweather..Miss
Probe........Mr. FOSTER | WALDRON
Cropley........Mr. CRISP | Miss Becby..Mrs. LEONARD
James..Mr. W. REMINGTON | Dinah Cropley.Mrs. HUMBY
Postilions....Messrs. Nichols and Adcock.

THE PALMY DAYS

In the course of the Evening Mr. HARLEY will introduce the following COMIC SONGS:
Manager Strut and his Comical Family.
THE HUMOURS OF A PLAYHOUSE;
or, PUNS IN WARM WEATHER.
" Waiter, bring another Bottle."
And the POPULAR SONG, WRITTEN EXPRESSLY FOR HIM, from "Cry To-Day and Laugh To-Morrow," called—
Veluti in Speculum ; or, The Stage and Green Room, In which he will introduce IMITATIONS
Of Mr. FAWCETT, Mr. KEMBLE, Mr. BLANCHARD, Mr. DE CAMP, and Mr. MATHEW'S EXORDIUM from
MAIL COACH ADVENTURES.
After which (first Time here) a popular Petite Piece, in One Act, called—

IS HE JEALOUS?

Mr. Belmour..Mr. CARTER	Harriet....Mrs. STANLEY
Mrs.Belmour Mrs. LEONARD	Rose ...... Mrs. HUMBY

An IRISH LILT, by Miss GREEN.
To which will be added (the second Time here) the popular Farce of—

Frighten'd to Death.

Phantom .... Mr. HARLEY	Mumps (his Servant)..
Carleton .... Mr. CARTER	Mr. CRISP
Colonel Bluff..	Emily .... Miss DIDDEAR
Mr. REMINGTON	Corinna....Mrs. LEONARD
Sir Joshua Greybeard..	Patty ...... Mrs. HUMBY
Mr. FOSTER	

THE PALMY DAYS

☛ Doors to be opened at Six, and to begin precisely at Seven o'clock.
Boxes, 4s.—Pit, 2s.—Gallery, 1s.——Second Price, Boxes, 2s.—Pit, 1s.
₊ Tickets and Places to be had of Mr. HOPE, at the Theatre, from Eleven till One.

By Desire of Mr. and Mrs. WENTWORTH, on Friday, Sept. 5th,
Guy Mannering; and The Broken Sword.

Fitzgerald died the following spring. The inscription on his tombstone in the churchyard at St. John's, Wakefield, is as follows :—

"Here lieth the mortal remains of R. J. Fitzgerald, Esq., late Manager of the theatres attached to the York circuit. He departed this life the 31st of May, 1818, in the forty-fifth Year of his Age. Monarchs, Sages, Peasants, must follow thee, and come to Dust."

On the 26th August, 1818, the theatre opened under new management.

"The melancholy and deeply to be lamented death of Mr. Fitzgerald having rendered it necessary for some one to undertake the conducting of the concern, Mr. Mansel is induced, from his friendship for the deceased, and his regard for Mr. Fitzgerald's Representatives, to forego his intention of retiring from the profession, and to devote his time to the arduous undertaking of managing the theatres during the remainder of the lease as the deputy of Mrs. and Miss Fitzgerald. He feels but too deeply the responsibility of the situation he is placed in, and candidly acknowledges his great inferiority to his predecessor. He dares not compare with him in any one thing—save his desire to please and his anxiety to do right. Mr. Mansel conceives it but fair and candid to state that his late friend, with all the enterprise and spirit which marked his character, embarked the whole of his property in the precarious and uncertain pursuit of profits to arise from a seven years' lease—his expenditure upon entering it was considerable—the times very unfavourable —and he was looking up to his exertions for the last three years of his term for remuneration. It was the divine will of Heaven that he should be deprived of that satisfaction. With the hope of still securing the advantages to the Widow and Orphan, Mr. Mansel, with all respect solicits the aid and approbation of those, who, perhaps, under other circumstances would be indifferent to the progress of the concern; and he begs leave to assure them that nothing shall be wanting on his part (within his power) to render the theatre as attractive as possible; and he will not entertain a doubt when the merits of the case are examined by the benevolent and the liberal, but that the event will be crowned with approval and success."

THE PALMY DAYS

Robert Mansel, like his predecessor Wilkinson, had plunged into the perils of print. His work, published in 1814, was a contribution to the ancient and bootless controversy as to whether the drama be but a wile of that Personage who is reported to have himself once acted the part of a serpent with considerable success. Wilkinson had occasionally descended into this arena, and broken a lance with the Prynnes of his day; but if his literary efforts had consisted wholly of such passages at arms (as Mansel's book does) they would hardly possess the interest they have at the present day. Another fact about Mansel worth mentioning is that he appears to have been a member of the company in which W. C. Macready made his first appearance at Birmingham in 1810. *The Wakefield and Halifax Journal* thus speaks of his first season of management:—

"The Theatre at Wakefield opened on Wednesday under the management of Mr. Mansel, who appears determined to tread in the spirited and liberal steps of his lamented friend and predecessor. The changes that have taken place in the *dramatis personæ* (*sic*) as far as we have yet been able to judge have not been for the worse. The aggregate of talent as well as numbers appears indisputably to be augmented, even in the regular corps; but whilst Mrs. Garrick remains amongst them a treat is offered to the lovers of the drama not easily to be exceeded, but especially to those who are 'moved by the concert (*sic*) of sweet sounds.' If displays of activity delight any, Mr. Wilson certainly offers to them a gratification no other is able to bestow, as he is confessedly esteemed the first performer on the rope now in Europe."

This Mrs. Garrick played Rosina in the "musical farce" of that name, Carline in *The Young Hussar* and Ophelia. Other plays performed this year were *Much Ado about Nothing*, for Mansel's benefit; *Adelgitha, The Rivals, The Innkeeper's Daughter, Pizarro, The Ravens, or the Force of Conscience, The Conquest of Torento, or the Fall of Tunis, Bellamira*, and amongst the after-pieces, *The Day after the Wedding, Of Age To-morrow, Raising the Wind,*

THE PALMY DAYS

and X.Y.Z. Whether the "first performer on the rope in Europe" wheeled a barrow from the stage up to the gallery between the acts of *Hamlet* I am not aware, but this feat is advertised during the season.

And now (1819) comes the appearance at the Wakefield Theatre of "the greatest genius that our stage has ever seen"—Edmund Kean. "In Shylock," says Mr. Henry Irving, comparing Kean with Garrick and John Kemble, "in Richard, in Iago, and, above all, in Othello, it may be doubted whether Edmund Kean ever had an equal." Richard and Othello were the two characters in which he appeared at Wakefield on the 16th and 17th July. It was his representation of the former that occasioned Coleridge's well-known saying that to see Kean act was like reading Shakespeare by flashes of lightning; and Hazlitt considered his Othello to be the finest piece of acting ever exhibited. The Wakefield playgoers therefore had an opportunity of seeing the "great little man" in two of his best parts, and at a period when he was himself at his best; but, for some reason or other, the theatre was not, says the paper, "so full as we anticipated, particularly on the second night."

In the autumn the Wakefield Theatre was the scene of the "first appearance on any public stage" of Miss Bakewell, a young lady who was a native of the town. Mr. Henry Clarkson says, in his pleasant *Memories of Merry Wakefield*, that she was pretty, as young ladies (especially in memories) are apt to be, and in this he is corroborated by contemporary records. She chose for her *début* (August 23rd) Belvidera in *Venice Preserved*, and between that date and September 3rd she played lead in four other tragedies—Mrs. Haller in *The Stranger*, Mrs. Beverley in *The Gamester*, Isabella in *The Fatal Marriage*, and Evadne in Shiel's drama of that name. The latter had

THE PALMY DAYS

but lately been produced with Miss O'Neill* in the title rôle—an actress of much charm and pathos, in whose footsteps, it is said, Miss Bakewell aspired to tread. It is unfortunate that there remains no more critical account of the artistic result of a brave beginning than the notices which appeared in the Wakefield paper. These are confessedly from the pen of a personal friend, who says a great many nice things, informing us that in Miss Bakewell, "dignity, innocence, and beauty are sweetly blended together," and expressing an earnest desire that the most fragile of these qualities might be long preserved. He adds, however, that "a new star has arisen in the histrionic firmament, shedding at its first rise a peculiarly pleasing lustre, and . . . when it shall have

---

* Mr. Clarkson says, "I perfectly recollect seeing lovely Miss O'Neill—afterwards Lady Becher—as Juliet on our Wakefield Boards;" and I am sorry I have not come across the record of her appearance. She had retired from the stage on July 13th, 1819.

advanced to its meridian height it will be found to be a star of the first magnitude;" from which metaphor we may no doubt infer (what, indeed, we should have suspected without it) that Miss Bakewell's talents were rather undeveloped. The first appearance of a novice in parts already appropriated by more than one actress of the first rank seems to afford another contrast to our own day, when it is admitted that, however naturally gifted an aspirant may be, there is a technique in acting, as in every other form of artistic expression, only to be acquired by study and the endurance of more or less drudgery. I incline, however, to the opinion that this was an exceptional occasion even in 1819. But the theatre was filled with a friendly audience, and Mr. Mansel, the manager, who acted with the *débutante*, had little reason to complain of the business. The star, it is said, did not remain in the 'histrionic firmament' many years. Perhaps, like Miss

THE PALMY DAYS

O'Neill, it was ultimately extinguished by matrimony.

In 1820 James Wallack was at Wakefield for four nights, playing (August 30th) Rolla in *Pizarro*, (September 1st and 2nd) Macbeth and Coriolanus. He was a noted Shakespearean actor in his day, and afterwards went to America. Mr. Bancroft, in the entertaining book which contains the reminiscences of himself and his wife, writes that when he was at New York, in 1858, he had "the rare treat of seeing James Wallack—then a lame and crippled old man, but still very handsome—act as Don Cæsar de Bazan; also in Douglas Jerrold's *Rent Day*, and Shylock in a production of *The Merchant of Venice*." On the 4th September Miss Bakewell re-appeared for three nights as Juliet, and on the 11th Wallack acted Brutus in *The Fall of Tarquin* for his benefit. The lady's benefit was on the 8th, when, says *The Wakefield and Halifax Journal* :—

THE PALMY DAYS

"Our theatre presented one of the most numerous and brilliant audiences ever witnessed in it. Among the strangers we distinguished the Countess of Mexbro', Lady Pollington, Mr. and Lady E. Smyth, Lady Smith, Mrs. Beaumont and family, Mr. and Mrs. Wentworth and family, Mrs. Lee and family, Major and Mrs. Crowther, Mrs. Dodsworth, Sir Wm. Pilkington, Col. Smith, Miss Smith, Messrs. Stanhope, Beckett, &c., &c."

This "list of visitors" at least shows, that whatever may be the case with prophets, an actress, young, pretty, and somewhat inexperienced, is not without honour even in her own neighbourhood.

On May 19th, 1821, Mr. De Camp, "having formed an arrangement with Mrs. Fitzgerald for the remainder of her Lease," opened the theatre "with the conjoint Talent of the York and Newcastle-upon-Tyne Companies."

Mansel, of whose mastery of English I have already furnished one illustration, heralds the opening of the 1821 autumn season with another manifesto, in which, as he modestly puts it, "he

THE PALMY DAYS

is happy to say he has it in his power to present a Company of Ladies and Gentlemen possessing a considerable portion of Talent and Respectability." He proceeds to offer the following inducement :—

"Mr. Mansel, having on his first Night of Management issued Eleven Hundred Free Admissions for the York Theatre, and not wishing to be thought improperly impartial to one Town more than another, announces that it is his intention to distribute SEVEN HUNDRED on the *FIRST NIGHT of opening the Theatre at Wakefield,* which will be on THURSDAY, August 30th, 1821, when will be presented the Musical Play of *Guy Mannering*, and the Farce of *Raising the Wind.*"

The names of the ladies and gentlemen who possess the considerable portion of talent and respectability follow, and I give them as showing the extent of the Company:—Messrs. Calvert, Wilders, Prichard, Williams, Yarnold, Downe, Hammond, Rayner, Kelly, Andrews, Elston, Bland, Smith, Webster, Morelli, W. Remington, Bywater, Dumbleton; Mesdames Weston, Hume,

THE PALMY DAYS

Lennard, Darley, Rayner, Andrews, Webster, French; Misses Chester, Johnson, Hague, Scruton, Green; Treasurer, Mr. Hope ('a good name,' as Touchstone says); Prompter, Mr. Remington; Leader of the Band, Mr. Jackson; Scene Painter, Mr. Willis; Head Carpenter, Mr. Bailes; Dress Makers, Mr. Ward and Miss Bearpark. "N.B.—The Theatre is new painted and decorated."

Mathews, the entertainer, visited the theatre again in October, after the theatrical season.

In May, 1822, the theatre opened for two nights with "A Pageant of the Coronation of His Majesty George the Fourth," which had taken place the year before. "The attempt in this Representation," runs the advertisement, "is, as far as Stage Limits will allow, to present a faithful Delineation of the various local Paraphernalia and Decorations beheld on that occasion." There were four scenes. First, "The Royal Procession, passing from the Hall

THE PALMY DAYS

to the Abbey." Second, "The Interior of Westminster Abbey, Galleries fitted up for the Reception of Foreign Princes, Ambassadors, and their Ladies. The Crown, the Altar, Throne of Homage, Coronation Chair of St. Edward, Regalia, &c., &c." Third, "Birdcage Walk in St. James' Park, with Introductory Dialogue interspersed with Songs." And fourth, "Interior of Westminster Hall, prepared for the Royal Banquet. In the course of the scene, the Grand Entree of the King's Champion, in complete Armour, mounted on a real Charger, richly caparisoned. The Ceremony of giving the Challenge and receiving the Gold Cup from the King." Elliston had appeared at Drury Lane in a pageant of this kind.

The usual season in the autumn followed (August 29th to September 14th). The plays given (omitting the minor pieces) were *The Castle of Andalusia*, *Mary Stuart*, *Mirandola*, Colman's *Law of Java*, *Virginius*, *The Pirate*,

THE PALMY DAYS

The Illustrious Travellers, Jane Shore, Wallace, The Suspicious Husband, The Jealous Wife, Othello, and *The Marriage of Figaro.*

The following year (1823) the theatre did not open for the regular season until October 20th. On this date W. J. Hammond, "from the Theatre Royal, Haymarket," made "his first appearance" at Wakefield, playing Bob Acres. He afterwards made a great hit as Sam Weller at the Strand, and joined Macready at Covent Garden in 1837. A few days later, on the 27th October, was performed, "under the Patronage of Godfrey Wentworth Wentworth, Esq., and Mrs. Wentworth, *George Heriot, or the Fortunes of Nigel,* with the farce of *Catharine and Petruchio,*" a somewhat curious arrangement of the respective works of Walter Scott and William Shakespeare; and on the 30th, *Twelfth Night,* announced as "not acted here these forty years."

On the 16th October, 1824, Robert Mansel

THE PALMY DAYS

died on the road to London, whither he was proceeding on business. On the 22nd the following appeared in the *Journal*:—

"The Nobility, Gentry, and Public of Wakefield and the Vicinity are most respectfully informed that their late worthy and deeply regretted Manager, Mr. Mansel, having made every arrangement for the period of his intended absence, the Business of the Theatre will be resumed on Monday next, October 25th, 1824, when it is humbly hoped that the Ladies and Gentlemen of the Establishment, in addition to their irreparable loss, may not experience any diminution of that Public Patronage and Support which has ever been their most anxious wish to acquire, and under the present melancholy circumstances will be their only consolation to preserve."

The season ended November 13th. In 1825 the Wakefield stage was occupied for a night or two by amateurs, by leave of Messrs. Downe and Faulkner, the successors of Mansel in the management. They played *The Castle Spectre*, by M. G. Lewis, and, by way of a change from the supernatural, *The Rivals*. The following spring the members of the Shakespeare Society gave two performances for the benefit of the

THE PALMY DAYS

Dispensary, choosing to appear, not as one would have supposed, in *Hamlet*, but in *John Bull* and *The Iron Chest*, both by George Colman the younger. This surely is a remarkable and praiseworthy instance of reverence for the bard. The theatre opened as usual October 30th, 1826, until the middle of November, during which time some fifteen dramas were played, besides farces. Amongst them were the lugubrious *George Barnwell*, *Romeo and Juliet*, *The School for Scandal*, *The Talisman*, *Paul Pry* (twice), *The Pilot* (twice), *The Hypocrite* (descended indirectly from *Tartuffe*), the well-worn *Isabella*, *John Bull*, *Douglas*, and *The Innkeeper's Daughter*.

On the 2nd June, 1827, Miss Maria Foote, of the Theatre Royal, Covent Garden, who married the Earl of Harrington four years later, appeared at Wakefield for one night in *The Belle's Stratagem*. The bill on this occasion is an interesting one :—

THE PALMY DAYS

Theatre, Wakefield.

FOR ONE NIGHT ONLY.

MR. DOWNE, anxious to provide every Novelty in his power for the amusement of his Patrons and Friends, has the gratification of announcing

MISS FOOTE,

Of the Theatre Royal, Covent Garden,

Whom he has engaged FOR ONE NIGHT ONLY, her previous arrangements precluding the possibility of her remaining any longer in this County.

On SATURDAY EVENING, *June 2nd, 1827,*
Will be performed the Comedy of the

BELLE'S STRATAGEM.

Doricourt, Mr. HEILD *(From the Theatre Royal, Bristol, his first appearance).*
Hardy, Mr. DOWNE. Sir G. Touchwood, Mr. CALVERT.
Flutter....Mr. W. J. HAMMOND.
Saville..Mr. PHELPS. Villers..Mr. WEBSTER.
Courtall......Mr. SELBY *(His first appearance here).*
First Gentleman....Mr. DEARLOVE.
Second Gentleman.............Mr. HAMILTON.
Mountebank........Mr. W. REMINGTON.

Letitia Hardy...........MISS FOOTE.

IN WHICH SHE WILL INTRODUCE THE POPULAR BALLAD OF
" Where are you going, my Pretty Maid?"

THE PALMY DAYS

And in the Masquerade Scene she will introduce the very favourite New Song of
"FOLLOW, FOLLOW, OVER MOUNTAIN."
Mrs. Racket..Miss PELHAM *(From the Theatre Royal, Exeter)*.
Lady Frances....Miss SEYMOUR.
Miss Ogle. Mrs. ANDREWS. Kitty Willis, Mrs. WEBSTER.
Ladies....Mesdames Bedford, Webster, &c.

TO CONCLUDE WITH THE FARCE OF
Of Age To-Morrow.
Frederick Baron Willinghurst, Mr. W. J. HAMMOND.
Baron Piffleberg, Mr. KELLY. Hans Molkus, Mr. DOWNE.
Friz....Mr. W. REMINGTON.
Maria..................MISS FOOTE.

IN WHICH SHE WILL SING
"OH! NO, MY LOVE, NO!"
And introduce a
NATIONAL MEDLEY DANCING SONG,
Written and arranged expressly for her.
Lady Brumback............Mrs. MACNAMARA.
Sophia......Miss SEYMOUR.
Places for the Boxes may be taken at Mr. NICHOLS', Bookseller.

Doors to open at Six o'Clock, and to commence at Seven.
Tickets—Boxes, 4s.; Pit, 2s.; Gallery, 1s.

R. NICHOLS, TYPOGRAPHER, WAKEFIELD.

THE PALMY DAYS

Before the opening of the theatre in October, Mr. Faulkner appears to have died, leaving Downe sole manager. We find again a notable name in the caste of *Jane Shore*, given the first night, October 29th — Belmour, Mr. Phelps, "from the Theatre Royal, Brighton." Shakespeare is better represented amongst the plays this season, *Romeo*, *Macbeth*, *The Merchant of Venice*, and "the afterpiece" of *Catherine and Petruchio* all appearing in the list, with *The Rivals*, *The Wonder*, *The School for Grown Children*, *George Barnwell*, and *Paul Pry* again, *Bombastes Furioso*, *The Devil among the Doctors*, and Morton's *Speed the Plough*, in which play, it will be remembered, that mysterious and influential lady, Mrs. Grundy, was first alluded to.

Towards the end of March, 1828, Downe "kindly lent" (the advertisement says) the theatre to Mr. Neville, "formerly of the York Company," and he brought down Mrs. Glover,

THE PALMY DAYS

Miss M. Glover, and W. J. Hammond. This celebrated actress played Mrs. Oakley in *The Jealous Wife* (March 25th), Violante in *The Wonder* to Hammond's Lissardo (28th), and Mrs. Malaprop in *The Rivals*, Hammond, of course, being Acres, and Miss Glover, Lydia (29th). Then we have, during April and May, the old, old story of *Romeo and Juliet* again, *The Slave, Bertram, High Life below Stairs, A New Way to Pay Old Debts;* "that moral and instructive lesson," as the bill styles it, *Thirty Years of a Gambler's Life, Gil Blas, Faustus, William Tell,* and others.

In September the theatre was opened for a fortnight by Mr. Cummins, who made a speech on the last night, in which "he hoped it might be the commencement of a long and, he trusted, prosperous season of unremitting efforts on his part and a continuance on theirs of that liberal support," &c., &c. During the twelve nights' season twenty-four pieces and after-pieces and a

THE PALMY DAYS

concert had been given. They included *Wild Oats, The Dramatist, The Way to get Married, The Siege of Belgrade, The Road to Ruin, Othello, Macbeth, Rob Roy, The Two Friends, The Steward*, and amongst the farces, *The Rencontre, 23, John Street, Adelphi*, and such old friends as *The Weathercock, Love Law and Physic*, and *Raising the Wind*. The following autumn (1829) Cummins let the Theatre to Mr. Butler, "of the Theatre, Sheffield," who opened on Monday, September 21st, with the old play of *Venice Preserved*, the part of Belvidera by Miss Smithson, "from the Theatre Royal, Covent Garden, and the Theatre Anglaise, Paris." This was "la belle Henriette" Smithson, who, with Liston, Charles Kemble, Macready, and others, had two years previously appeared in the French capital, and captivated the Parisians. There she had inspired the youthful Berlioz with that romantic passion which resulted in at least one symphony and one attempt at suicide. In 1833

THE PALMY DAYS

she was again in Paris, heard the symphony, and was introduced to the composer, who was not personally known to her, though she had received from him during her previous visit divers ardent communications. They were in a short time duly married, and he was as unhappy ever afterwards as genius, at least, usually is under the circumstances, whilst she inspired, at any rate, no more symphonies. However, *revenons à nos moutons.* On the 22nd September, 1829, Miss Smithson played Juliet, and Catherine in *Catherine and Petruchio*; on the 23rd, Imogene in *Bertram*, and Sophia in *The Rendezvous;* on the 24th, Mrs. Haller in *The Stranger*, and Lady Freelove in *The Day after the Wedding;* on the 25th, the name-part in *Jane Shore*, Portia in the fourth act of *The Merchant of Venice*, and Sophia again; and on the 26th, Violante in *The Wonder*, and Ella in *Ella Rosenberg*—a good week's work.

Calvert, still with the company, repeated his

THE PALMY DAYS

lectures on elocution during the season. In October an infant phenomenon called Master Burke played Richard III, and led the orchestra in the overture. This precocious youth sometimes played in three pieces in one evening. In November Butler engaged Madame Vestris for two nights, "the first of which will be on Friday, November 13th, 1829, when will be acted the new Musical Comedy of *The Rencontre*, the part of Justine by Madame Vestris... After which a farce called *All at Coventry*. The whole to conclude with the admired Burletta of *Midas*. Apollo, Madame Vestris. On Saturday, November 14th, A New Drama (never acted here) written expressly for the display of Madame Vestris's extraordinary talents, called *Sublime and Beautiful*. Charlotte, Madame Vestris. After which a new comic Interlude called *A Dead Shot*. To conclude with the popular Farce of *The One Hundred Pound Note*. Miss Arlington, Madame Vestris, as originally performed by her at the Theatre Royal, Covent Garden, and in which she introduces her original and popular song of *Buy a Broom*, in the costume of an Itinerant Bavarian Female. In consequence of the demand for places two rows of seats from the pit will be added to the boxes."

A " laughable interlude" called *The Married Bachelor* appears to have been substituted on this occasion for *The Dead Shot*, and to have greatly shocked the local critic. "The eternal repetition," he says, "of oscular salutations going forward upon the stage was, we know, not a little offensive to the more cultivated and modest part of the audience." Kissing—as a spectacle—is without doubt a somewhat unsatisfactory entertainment.

On the 16th November, Miss Bartolozzi, Madame Vestris's sister, played in *John of Paris*, and between the pieces Butler delivered 'a defence of the acted drama.' On the 25th

THE PALMY DAYS

January, 1830, Sheridan Knowles, the dramatist, began a course of lectures on *Belles Lettres* at the Music Saloon; this may perhaps be mentioned, though strictly it concerns not the theatre. The latter opened again in March, during which month Mr. Wood, "Principal Vocalist at the Theatre Royal, Covent Garden," appeared in opera—*The Quaker, Love in a Village*, and *The Devil's Bridge*—and the usual stock dramas were played. In August, Madame Vestris returned for one night, acting Phœbe in *Paul Pry* and Kate O'Brien in the farce of *Perfection;* and on September 18th, Rayner and Calvert gave their entertainment, including imitations of Kean, Young, and Kemble. W. J. Hammond had now assumed the management, and he continued to have it for a year or two. On January 25th, 1831, Edmund Kean appeared as Shylock—the character in which he had made his *début* at Drury Lane but one day short of seventeen years before, and to which,

THE PALMY DAYS

it will be remembered, he was the first actor to give a touch of pathos. At this time—only a little more than two years before his death—Kean was not what he had been; and the local newspaper gentleman, in a notice alluding to his previous visit to Wakefield, is shocked—this time with reason—at the lamentable and premature decay of the tragedian's powers. A copy of the playbill on this interesting evening is given here:—

Theatre, Wakefield.

MR. W. J. HAMMOND

Respectfully informs the Public that he has concluded an Engagement with the CELEBRATED TRAGEDIAN,

Mr. KEAN,

FOR ONE NIGHT ONLY, which will commence on the termination of his Engagement in Leeds, where he is now performing this present Week.

On TUESDAY, JANUARY 25th, 1831,
WILL BE PRESENTED SHAKESPEARE'S
MERCHANT OF VENICE.
Shylock......MR. KEAN.
Duke of Venice............Mr. DEARLOVE.

THE PALMY DAYS

Bassanio....(His first appearance here)..Mr. KEPPELL.
Antonio....Mr. WEBSTER
(His first appearance here these three years).
Gratiano..(His first appearance)..Mr. MELVILLE.
Lorenzo....Mr. JERROLD.   Launcelot..Mr. SLAITER.
Tubal......Mr. ANDREWS.
Salanio..Mr. JONES.   Old Gobbo..Mr. SMITH.
Portia....Miss PENLEY.
Nerissa....Miss ANGELL   Jessica....Miss MEARS.

The Performance to conclude with a Laughable Farce, called

Fortune's Frolic.

Old Smocks.............Mr. WEBSTER.
Franks....Mr. DEARLOVE.   Rattle....Mr. MELVILLE.
Clown..Mr. JERROLD.   Countryman..Mr. CULLEN.
Servant, Mr. SMITH.   Robin Roughhead, Mr. SLAITER.
Miss Nancy..Miss MEARS.   Dolly..Miss ANGELL.
Margery....Mrs. MACNAMARA.

⁎ Notwithstanding the HEAVY EXPENSE attending this Engagement,
NO ALTERATION WILL BE MADE IN THE PRICES.

BOXES, 4s.; PIT, 2s.; GALLERY, 1s.   Second Price:—
BOXES, 2s.; PIT, 1s.

☞ Places to be had of Mr. NICHOLS, Bookseller.
Doors to open at SIX, and the Performance to commence at SEVEN.
THE THEATRE WILL BE WELL AIRED.

RICHARD NICHOLS, TYPOGRAPHER, WAKEFIELD.

THE PALMY DAYS

The autumn season began October 17th. Upon two evenings the elder Mathews gave his entertainments — on the 22nd his "*Comic Annual*," and on the 26th his "*Sketch Book for 1830*, with humorous Cuts and other embellishments, Published this day (Boards) Wakefield (Packed in Boxes) Four Shillings." The humour of this seems to-day a little laboured, for, though Mr. Mathews's Sketches were 'published' on the boards of the theatre, it was the audience who (I hope) were packed in the boxes. On the 24th October there was another Coronation Pageant, this time of William IV. and Queen Adelaide. In May, 1832, Mr. and Mrs. Wood, of the Theatres Royal, Drury Lane and Covent Garden, appeared for three nights in opera. They played Hawthorn and Rosetta in *Love in a Village*, and Tom Tug and Wilhelmina in *The Waterman*, May 11th; Masaniello and Elvira in *Masaniello*, and Steady (one of Incledon's parts) and Gillian in *The Quaker*,

THE PALMY DAYS

May 12th; and Francis Osbaldiston and Diana Vernon in *Rob Roy*, with *The Quaker* again, on the 15th. Mr. Wood afterwards built and resided at Woolley Moor House, near Wakefield.

The following September Mr. Yates, "part. proprietor of The Theatre Royal, Adelphi, with Mr. Mathews," appeared for one night only, giving imitations of Young as Hamlet, Kean as Richard, Munden as Polonius, Macready as Virginius, Braham as Prince Orlando, and of Messrs. Yates and Mathews as themselves.

Hammond was succeeded as manager in 1833 by Mr. Read, who opened at Wakefield on the 18th November. Braham appeared in the opera of *Guy Mannering* on December 14th, and the house was open continuously until January 21st, 1834. The usual stock dramas were given — *The Iron Chest*, *Eugene Aram*, *Zembuca*, *The Hunchback*, *The Stranger*, &c.— and a Vocal and Instrumental Concert just before Christmas; but the fact that towards the

THE PALMY DAYS

end of the season "half-price nights" were occasionally advertised, seems to show that business was bad. And when the theatre re-opened, early in February, "half-price every night from commencement until further notice," appeared upon the bills. They finished the season, February 27th, with "a grand Masquerade and Fancy Ball" after the play, when it was announced that "those who purchase Box tickets will be entitled to join in the Masquerade"; and the theatre was open for three nights in May, when a young lady named Fanny Edwin, "twelve years of age," played Richard III. and Bombastes Furioso!

Such were the entertainments provided at the Wakefield Theatre in the days when, as old people tell us, the carriages of "the Nobility and Gentry" extended from its doors in unbroken line to the bottom of Westgate. It now only remains to continue these notes down to our own time.

V.
CONTINUATION AND DECADENCE.

The third day comes a frost—a killing frost.
Henry VIII.

ROUGHLY speaking, the beginning of the reign of our present Sovereign marks the rise of a new movement in English stagecraft. In 1837 Macready 'commenced manager' at Covent Garden, and began to give that attention to the minute details of theatrical representation, to the completeness and *vraisemblance* of a play as an artistic whole, which has culminated in our day in the unequalled stage management of such men as Mr. Irving and Mr. Hare. In the natural course of things it would be long before this movement, not very pronounced, perhaps, at the start, even in

CONTINUATION

London, affected the less important provincial theatres; but the period seems a convenient one at which to begin our last section, especially as about this time the Wakefield Theatre opened under a new manager, Mr. Joseph Smedley, who, as already mentioned, purchased the property himself a few years later.

Apropos of Macready, Dr. Wright, whose knowledge of Wakefield goes back more than sixty years, writes me "I feel almost certain that I once saw Macready on the Wakefield stage, though I cannot find mention of it in my diary; and I think he played Mr. Beverley in *The Gamester.*"

Mr. Smedley, manager of the Theatres, Beverley, Pontefract, Gainsboro', &c., opened at Wakefield, November 10th, 1835. Like a good many other people connected with the stage, he was, I have heard, originally occupied with the somewhat less fascinating pursuit of the law. I suppose, as he married an actress,

AND DECADENCE

love had turned him into an actor, even as it made a painter of the Antwerp blacksmith. He had two sons and two daughters in the profession —all of them in his company; and their names constantly appear in the Wakefield playbills from 1835 to 1841. He seems to have had a good opinion of the dignity of dramatic art, and the bills under his administration begin with solemn little essays about it.

That for instance, of the 23rd November, 1836, reads as follows :—

"The business of plays is to discountenance vice and commend virtue, to shew the uncertainty of human greatness, the sudden turns of fate, and the unhappy conclusions of violence and injustice; it is to expose the singularities of pride and fancy, to make folly and falsehood contemptible, to bring hypocrisy and everything that is ill under infamy and neglect. The wit of man cannot invent anything more conducive to virtue and destructive to vice than the drama."*

Another bill (November 2nd, 1840) presents

* This is a quotation from Jeremy Collier—a hostile witness, and proportionately effective.

CONTINUATION

us with the following information, in front of the caste of a drama so conducive to virtue as *The Honeymoon.*

"There is not perhaps within the range of social amusements one more worthy of our intellectual powers than this: and certainly none more replete with great variety, or endowed with more fascinating charms. The Theatre is the Temple of Arts, and in no place is their influence more deeply felt. All civilized communities have invariably been anxious to promote the welfare of the National Theatres, and precisely at those periods when refinement has been carried to the highest pitch has this solicitude most generally prevailed. At the very orgin of its institution, the sages of Greece were found among the promoters of Theatricals: and with very few exceptions, the greatest and wisest men of all countries have from that time to the present been patrons. And surely, none but those who would deny us amusements of every kind, and indiscriminately denounce any enjoyments (however lawful or innocent) could prohibit a recreation like this, which gives so wide a scope for the exercise and display of the highest faculties of the mind, and which at the same time presents so rich a combination of intellectual delight."

To con these sentences between the acts could not but have been grateful and comforting

AND DECADENCE

to the audience, and calculated to allay the qualms of the weaker brethren amongst them. Sometimes the manager waxes metaphorical, as thus—prefixed to the bill of 28th November, 1835 :—

"THE PERPETUAL COMEDY.

The World is the Stage—Men are the Performers—Chance composes the Piece—Fortune distributes the Parts—The Fools shift the Scenery—The Rich occupy the Boxes—The Powerful have their seat in the Pit, and the Poor sit in the Gallery—The Fair Sex present the Refreshments—The Trusty occupy the Treasury Benches (!) and those forsaken by Lady Fortune snuff the Candles—Folly makes the Concert and Time drops the Curtain—."

He also informs the public that " Monday Evening's Performance will be appropriated to opera, Wednesday, legitimate comedy (and set apart as the Fashionable Night,) Fridays, to melodrama and spectacle, and Saturdays, to tragedy." On the 31st December, 1836, when everyone in the house would be making good resolutions for the New Year, the following tract

CONTINUATION

is appropriately set forth before the caste of *George Barnwell*:—

A story is recorded, and the facts can be proved by many living witnesses, that a young gentleman in the City of London, having embezzled a part of his master's property, was providentially at a representation of *George Barnwell* at Drury Lane, when that admirable actor Mr. Ross personated the character of George Barnwell, at whose fate he was so struck to the soul that it occasioned his immediate contrition and reformation. The gentleman so benefitted by this excellent Tragedy was not ashamed to acknowledge his obligation to the play and the performer: for at every subsequent yearly benefit of Mr. Ross he always received one hundred pounds sterling with a card to the following effect— Dear Sir — One who is indebted to your admirable representation of George Barnwell for more than life, for his redeemed honour and credit, begs your acceptance of the enclosed, which you will receive yearly as long as you continue in the line of your profession. Happy am I to acknowledge that the stage has preserved me from ruin and disgrace. *George Barnwell* stopt me in my mad career and saved me from an ignominious death. I am your grateful friend and servant—"

It reads now rather more like the advertisement of a patent medicine than a play, but apparently in some such light the worthy man who at this time held the helm of the Wakefield theatrical ship regarded the drama. He tells us on another playbill that it "exercises all the kinder emotions, and by its influence over the mind and feelings prevents that moral stagnation which so often tends to degrade and *brutify*." "It should ever be his study," he said, in returning thanks to the public at the close of the 1837 season, "to make the Theatre both by precept and practice what its advocates contend for—A school of eloquence, a temple of the arts, the shrine of the muses, the chastener of our morals, and the mild but persuasive monitress of our duties." 'Art for art's sake' was then an unknown doctrine. These flourishes are characteristic of the time, though the kind of person is by no means yet extinct who, whilst taking his pleasure, desires to be persuaded that he is simultaneously improving his mind or his morals. Mr. Smedley not only professed to

CONTINUATION

cater for this class, but "founded his claim for support not on the Professional Talent of his Company only, but what to him has ever been deemed of the first importance, the Rectitude of their Conduct." This, it must be admitted, was going quite as far as most managers would care to go. In his later years he settled at Sleaford, and became a printer and bookseller.

During the 1835 season, from November 10th to the beginning of January, 1836, were played *George Barnwell, Speed the Plough, Town and Country, Guy Mannering, Pizarro, The Castle Spectre, Jane Shore, Romeo, Ivanhoe, The Heart of Midlothian, The Heir at Law* (under the patronage of " The Young Gentlemen of the Proprietary School "), *Married Life, Macbeth, The Merchant of Venice, She Stoops to Conquer, The Water Witch, The Hunchback*, and others. A full list of the 1836-7 season has already been given.

Of Smedley's two daughters, the younger,

AND DECADENCE

Miss Annette Smedley, had the greater liking for the stage, and played more important parts than her sister. Ophelia, Belvidera, Rebecca in *Ivanhoe*, and Lady Teazle are amongst the characters she sustained during the season of 1836. Miss Smedley, the elder sister, played boys' parts, such as the Prince of Wales in *Richard III.*, and Paul in *The Wandering Boys*, or girls masquerading as boys, such as Viola. She shared this particular line, however, with a young lady, apparently of great vivacity and versatility, named Desborough, who, besides taking the second boys, dancing hornpipes 'between,' and impersonating the Mrs. Rattletons and Louisa Lovetricks in all the farces, played such parts as Virginia in Sheridan Knowles's play, and Madeline Lester in *Eugene Aram*. It seems that Miss Desborough's charms made considerable havoc amongst the susceptible, and her admirers presented her on her benefit night (29th December, 1836,) with

CONTINUATION

"a splendid Gold Watch, Chain and Seals," when, as one who was present informs me, "she was dressed in white, and looked magnificent. The names of the Misses Smedley are absent from the bill on this presentation evening; and I believe Miss Desborough played no more at Wakefield after the end of that season. *Verb. sap.*

Smedley's management continued for several years, his family assisting him in the business. Sometimes one of the sons 'tripled' Osric, Rosencrantz, and the first Gravedigger on one evening, or, if not wanted on the stage, played second violin in the orchestra; and no doubt the old gentleman kept them all well employed. This domestic combination (and the rectitude of the Company's conduct) seem to have been sufficient attraction without the assistance of 'stars,' and I have not found any notable names in the bills until November, 1838, in which month Henry Betty, the son of the Infant

AND DECADENCE

Roscius, appeared as Selim in *Barbarossa*, as Alexander, and as Norval in *Douglas*, and Mr. Butler played Virginius, Hamlet, and William Tell. On December 5th, 1839, *Twelfth Night* was performed, with Miss Woolgar as Valentine, and Mr. Woolgar as Malvolio. Miss Smedley was the Viola, and Curio was also played by a girl, Miss Wilton. There was at Wakefield a child actress of that name, who, a few years later, recited epilogues and other dreadful things, the daughter of a Mr. and Mrs. Wilton, whose names now and then appear amongst those of the members of Smedley's Company; but as in 1842 she is described as five years of age, she could hardly, making all possible allowance for theatrical ages, have played Curio in 1839. Neither young lady must be mistaken for the Miss Wilton who afterwards became Mrs. Bancroft, and who kindly informs me she has no recollection of ever having been in Wakefield. Woolgar, of course, is a well-known

CONTINUATION

name, and so is Young—'Mr. Young, of the Theatre Royal, Drury Lane,'—who appeared on the 30th October, 1840, as Gloster, and during November and December as Damon in *Damon and Pythias*, Brutus in *The Fall of Tarquin*, Hamlet (for his benefit), Octavian in *The Mountaineers*, Alexander in *Alexander the Great*, Master Walter in *The Hunchback*, Bertram, Jacques in *As You Like It*, the Chevalier St. Franc in *The Point of Honour*, and Doricourt in *The Belle's Stratagem*. On the 22nd December we have *The Heir at Law*, Homespun, Mr. Rayner; Dick Dowlas, Mr. Bedford; and Doctor Pangloss, "LL.D. and A.S.S.," Mr. Smedley; and on the 23rd *The School of Reform*, Ferment, Mr. Bedford, and Tyke, Mr. Rayner. Both Bedford and Rayner were leading comedians in their day, and the latter had succeeded Emery in the representation of broad Yorkshire parts. Rayner appeared on the 24th as Giles in *The Miller's Maid*, Chip in *A Chip of the*

AND DECADENCE

Old Block, and Fixture in *A Roland for an Oliver*; and on the 26th as Harry Wakefield in *The Two Drovers*, and Paddock in *My Spouse and I*.

During the season, besides the above, *The Lady of Lyons*, *Naval Engagements*, *The Maid and the Magpie*, *The Honeymoon*, *The Love Chase*, the inevitable *George Barnwell*, with *Love, Law, and Physic, Raymond and Agnes*, and Sheridan Knowles's *Love* were presented. The nights of performing were still (as in 1836, except when Conservative Dinners dislocated the local theatrical universe) Monday, Wednesday, Friday, and Saturday. On the 30th December G. V. Brooke appeared as Othello; on the 1st January, 1841, and following nights, as Ravenswood, Rolla in *Pizarro*, Selim in *Barbarossa*, Romeo, and O'Callaghan in *His Last Legs;* and on the 9th, for his benefit, as Claude Melnotte, and Lieutenant Kingston in *Naval Engagements*.

CONTINUATION

The theatre opened again on May 26th, under the management of Mr. Hooper, of the York, Hull, and Leeds Theatres, who announced (rather late in the day) that he had "added the Wakefield Theatre to the York Theatrical Circuit," on which occasion Mr. Cathcart, of Covent Garden; Mr. King, of Drury Lane; Mr. Davidson, of "The Theatre Royal, English Opera, London;" and Mr. and Mrs. Hooper, "late of Drury Lane and Madame Vestris's Olympic Theatre," appeared. On Saturday, August 14th, the Adelphi Company visited Wakefield 'for one night only,' including Mr. and Mrs. Yates, Mrs. Hooper, Wright, Wieland, Lyon, and Paul Bedford. On the 23rd October Charles Kean played Hamlet to Mrs. Hooper's Ophelia. Dr. Wright relates, *apropos* of this visit of Kean's, how Hooper, the manager, called upon him to borrow a skull for the churchyard scene, and forgot to return it. As it was sawn in two horizontally through the forehead, as skulls

AND DECADENCE

intended for medical study are, it must have required careful handling on the part of Hamlet.

In May, 1842, Madame Celeste appeared as Madeline in *St. Mary's Eve*, and also in a piece called *The French Spy*, in which she and Mr. Pritchard executed a broad-sword combat—no doubt the exhilarating 'two up and two down' business of that day. Bedford was in this company, and Madame Celeste danced "*La Normande*" between the plays. On the 14th, Mr. and Mrs. Wood made "positively their last appearance," in *Fra Diavolo* and *The Waterman*.

On July 9th, *Rob Roy* and *Kate Kearney* were given, with Mr. and Mrs. Waylett and Bedford in the caste. Mrs. Waylett, "The Queen of English Ballad," as she is described, appeared at Wakefield more than once.

Early in 1844 the lessees of the theatre were Messrs. J. Mosley and Charles Rice, "successors to Mr. Smedley." Rice was for many years at a subsequent period the lessee of the Theatre Royal, Bradford, where he and his wife, who succeeded to the management of that house upon his death, were much respected. In March, 1845, Mr. and Miss Vandenhoff appeared at Wakefield again, in *Love's Sacrifice;* and, later in the month, Miss Charlotte Cushman, an American actress, who had a short time before made her first appearance in England. She and her sister Susan, it will be remembered, used to play Romeo and Juliet together.

At the commencement of the winter season, on December 2nd, this year, it is announced that "the stage will be lighted from above in the style of the London theatres." On December 29th was given *She Stoops to Conquer*— Hastings, Mr. Lewis Ball; Tony Lumpkin, Mr. C. Rice; concluding with a "Grand Comic Christmas Pantomime." Pantomimes did not yet occupy the whole of an evening. Rice was in after years celebrated for the production of

AND DECADENCE

this kind of entertainment, in the days, not so very long ago, when it still retained a semblance of dramatic form in the shape of a coherent plot, and in substance was primarily adapted for the amusement of those whom he calls "the younger branches." Mr. Ball is still, or very lately was, upon the road with the Comptons, playing all the old men in their repertory. I was glad to find an eulogy of this old actor, whom many of us have seen and admired, in an article in the Gentleman's Magazine for February last, by Mr. Percy Fitzgerald. "Nothing," writes Mr. Fitzgerald, "could be more natural, ripe, full, or convincing than his interpretations. Everything he did was correct, and gave pleasure."

On the 22nd February, 1847, Cherry's Comedy of *The Soldier's Daughter* was performed, the part of Frank Heartall by Mr. Sullivan, "of the Theatres Royal, Edinburgh and Glasgow." Wakefield was the first town

CONTINUATION

in England in which Barry Sullivan appeared, and he remained here during the season, playing (March 3rd) Matthew Elmore in Ford's *Love's Sacrifice*, (March 8th) Julius to Vandenhoff's Virginius, (March 9th) Bassanio to Vandenhoff's Shylock, (March 12th) The Ghost to Vandenhoff's Hamlet, (March 16th) Sir Edward Mortimer in Colman's *Iron Chest*, (March 19th) Julian in Sheridan Knowles's *The Wife*, (March 20th) Don Felix in Mrs. Centlivre's *The Wonder*, (March 22nd) Sir Giles Overreach in Massinger's *A New Way to Pay Old Debts*, (March 25th, for his benefit) Claude Melnotte and Don Felix, and (March 26th) Faulkland (part hated of actors) in *The Rivals*. On March 5th, Mude, of Drury Lane and Haymarket Theatres, played The Stranger to Mrs. Pollock's Mrs. Haller, and the next evening—which, by the way, was under the patronage of Mr. and Mrs. Joseph Wood, "of Woolley Moor," where they now resided—the

AND DECADENCE

same actor appeared in *The Honeymoon*, which was followed by *Boots at the George*.

In these days of constant new productions it is curious to notice the age of some of the plays in the above list. Excepting Shakespeare, who, of course, never grows old, *A New Way to Pay Old Debts* and *Love's Sacrifice* had been produced in 1620 and 1633 respectively: *The Wonder* had held the stage for more than a hundred and thirty years, and *The Iron Chest* since the end of the eighteenth century.

We have now arrived at that artistic, middle nineteenth century period which saw beauty in the crinoline, and amongst other ways of o'er stepping the modesty of nature, seems to have imagined that tragedy meant noise. I quote again from Mr. Fitzgerald's article.

"So firmly established is the reign of the romantic or realistic system, that it is difficult to conceive that only five-and-twenty years ago there were players who tore parts to tatters, and mouthed and churned their words. These gentry were acceptable, too, and followed. Such was the

CONTINUATION

late G. V. Brooke, who now seems to us somewhat of Mr. Crummles' pattern. Another of these protagonists, who was strangely popular and drew great houses, was the late Barry Sullivan, to see whom in the crook'd-backed Richard's fright— Cibber's version, *bien entendu*— was an amazing thing. Such roarings, gaspings, growlings and ferocious cuttings and drivings could not be conceived or described. Nor shall I forget his other dying agonies in *The Gamester*, protracted for an immense time. The poor gentleman lay on the floor, his family weeping round, whilst every instant he was projecting loud sustained groans. He writhed and rolled, conveying that the poison was actually doing its work, and that he was suffering frightful internal agonies. This sort of thing is now extinct."

May it rest in peace.

In February, 1851, Mr. Charles Pitt appeared in *Hamlet, Macbeth, Richard III., The Iron Chest, The Gamester, Ingomar, The Lady of Lyons*, and *Richelieu*, and the theatre opened again in September. *The Stranger* was given on the 3rd, and the attention of the audience is called by a line in the playbill to "the new act-drop, the Church of Santa Maria della Salute, Venice." It is also announced that a Ladies'

AND DECADENCE

Cloak Room is attached to the boxes. The principal performers in the company at this time were Prescott, Norman, W. P. Vaughan, H. Lacey, Wilton, and Misses Juliet Power and Marian Douglas; Stage Manager Mr. Reynolds. On the 23rd September was performed *Luke the Labourer*, and *The Merchant of Venice*, compressed into four acts and ending with the trial scene; on the 24th, *The Taming of the Shrew*, with the interlude of *No ! a Pas de Nation* by Miss Salmon, and the after-piece of *The Charcoal Burner*. This was under the patronage of Mr. and Mrs. J. Wood again. Other plays were *Charles of Sweden*, with *The Serious Family* (September 26th); *John Bull*, with *Bachelors' Buttons* (September 29th); and in October *The Mutiny at the Nore*, with *Tom Noddy's Secret*, and *The Married Rake*; *Robert Macaire*, with *The Flowers of the Forest*; *My Poll and my Partner Joe*, with *The Lottery Ticket*, and *Everyone has his Fault*, the

CONTINUATION

"bespeak" of the Medical Profession, who had already given their patronage one evening in March of this year.

The playbill of the 15th October drops into poetry:—

"The curtain will rise at seven o'clock, to Shakespeare's celebrated Tragedy of *King Lear*—

> The lapse of ages has no power upon thee,
> Save that like silver from the furnace blaze
> Each trial proves thee of superior value ! . . .

To conclude, by particular desire with the Fashionable Comedy, entitled *Nell Gwynne*."

And then, as if it were desirable to whitewash Nelly a little before presenting her to the unfashionable middle classes, it proceeds—

"This play is the production of one of the most graphic and caustic writers of the day and was merely written to shew some glimpses of the 'silver lining' of the character of Nell Gwynne, to whose influence over the Merry Monarch, Charles the Second, the English people owe a national asylum for veteran soldiers, and whose brightness shines with most amiable lustre in many actions of her extraordinary career—

> Princes may retire whene'er they please,
> And breathe free air from out their palaces ;
> They go sometimes unknown to shun their state,
> And then 'tis manners not to know or wait."

AND DECADENCE

Already there were signs that the theatre with difficulty kept up its ancient status. Even during Rice's administration he had to give notice "that persons entering the Theatre in a state of intoxication, smoking, throwing orange peel, nut shells, &c., shouting, or personally addressing the musicians or other individuals in the Theatre, or in any way disturbing or annoying the audience, will be instantly removed by the constables, who are in constant attendance to preserve order," and to stipulate that "season tickets for the Boxes for ten nights' performances can be obtained *if applied for by parties of known respectability.*" This is only the most specific of a series of similar warnings; and presently to threatened rowdyism 'in front' came rascality 'behind.' In 1855 appeared the bogus manager; and disappeared, as his manner is, on the eve of the 'treasury' day, leaving the unfortunate company in the lurch. Mr. Thorne, in announcing his intention to open the theatre

CONTINUATION

in May of that year, laments "the various failures that have lately taken place in theatrical speculation in the town of Wakefield. At this period Infant Phenomena and Strong Men "from the Crimea" filled up the numerous gaps in the managerial succession. Still the prices of admission were maintained, and on the 12th February, 1859, Charles Mathews appeared as Plumper in *Cool as a Cucumber*, The Chevalier in *The Comical Countess* (the Countess being played by Mrs. C. Mathews), and as Motley in *He would be an Actor*. And in the hands of Mr. Belton, the manager in 1859-60, whom Dr. Wright describes as "an educated, agreeable gentleman," the house enjoyed another season of prosperity. During 1859, *Ingomar*, *Macbeth*, *The Corsican Brothers*, followed by *Beauty and the Beast*, and concluding with *The Spectre Bridegroom*, *Rob Roy*, and *Faust* were put on. The *Express* of November 5th thus speaks of the season:—

AND DECADENCE

"Mr, Belton closed the season at Wakefield last evening . . . We have to congratulate him on leaving behind him a reputation which cannot fail to ensure him a cordial welcome when he again visits the town. He has conducted the theatre in an admirable manner, and has won golden opinions from all the patrons of the drama. He himself is a very superior actor, and his company are far above the average of provincial players . . . . . Mr. Belton took his benefit on Monday evening when the house was crowded. The season appropriately wound up with *Hamlet*, Mr. Belton performing in an admirable manner the part of the philosophic prince."

The theatre was open again in May and June, 1860, under Belton's management, and on the 8th of the latter month was played *She Stoops to Conquer*, followed by "a new farce called *Two Faces under One Hood*, written by a gentleman of Wakefield"—none other, I am informed, than Mr. George Atkinson, the present Town Clerk of Liverpool. On October 1st, Belton, who also gave readings in the Corn Exchange, opened the theatre for a six weeks' season, with a repertory including *The Wife*,

CONTINUATION

The Man with the Iron Mask, *To Oblige Benson*, *Ingomar*, and *Never Too Late to Mend*.

In March, 1862, Sir John Hay, M.P., patronized the theatre after the old fashion, when *The Power of Love* was in the bill, appropriately followed by *Betsy's Young Man*. The following year there were two amateur performances on February 4th and 6th, given by members of the Leeds Rifle Corps, assisted by Miss Weston, Miss Macready, and Miss Larkin. They interpreted on the first evening *The Merchant of Venice* and *The Very Latest Edition of the Lady of Lyons*, and on the second, *The Honeymoon* and *Boots at the Swan*.

Soon after this time, as stated in the first section, followed the beerhouse period, which can as well be imagined as described, and need not be either. The files of the local papers know the old theatre no more for many years. The decadence of some things is associated with much of beauty, but here is but a faint afterglow, and it came late.

AND DECADENCE

On the 17th December, 1883, "The place of public amusement in Westgate, formerly known as the Theatre Royal, but more recently as the Alhambra Music Hall," as the newspaper, with almost legal precision puts it, was opened by Mr. Sherwood, the new proprietor; "the interior renovated, and structurally altered, a dress circle provided, and the objectionable bar at the front of the building entirely removed." The circle, as already explained, was only a circle by courtesy, the house not having been (as the vulgar phrase is) built that way; neither was evening dress usually indispensable. But the alterations made were distinctly improvements, though principally confined to the entrance and staircases. The theatre was now styled the "Royal Opera House." *Storm Beaten*, a dramatised version of one of Robert Buchanan's novels, was given, with Edmund Tearle and his wife (Miss Kate Clinton) in the leading parts. During the first week in the

CONTINUATION

New Year the Carl Rosa Opera Company appeared in *The Bohemian Girl*, *Trovatore*, and *Carmen*, with Madame Marie Roze in the title rôle. For the next few years the management endeavoured to induce the better sort of playgoer to frequent the house, and during a week's engagement of Mr. Wilson Barrett's *Proof* Company in February, 1885, "distinguished patronage" was secured for two evenings. But it was too hopelessly out of date, both "in front" and "behind," and perhaps the memory of the "objectionable bar," which had to be crossed for nearly twenty years, was not easy to obliterate.

One of D'Oyley Carte's companies performed in *The Mikado* for two nights in the December following; but for the most part the fare provided may be described as Adelphian melodrama, tempered with the legitimate. *The Crimes of Paris*, *The House on the Marsh*, *Proved True*, *No Mercy*, *The New Magdalen*,

AND DECADENCE

The Colleen Bawn, East Lynne—to take a few names at random—with a "Shakespearian" week, wherein *The Taming of the Shrew* is played as an afterpiece to *The Stranger*—are all advertised about this time. The last occasion, probably, on which the pit was invaded by the boxes was when Miss Nancy Kemp Brammall, a Wakefield lady formerly well known as an amateur, played Mary Netley in *Ours* and Tilly in *School*, as a member of Mr. S. Austin's company. But this lapse of the Westgate stage into Robertsonian comedy was only a digression; more sensational pieces, of the class of which *The Two Orphans* and *The Grip of Iron* (both given at the Wakefield theatre during its last year or two) are perhaps about the best, better pleased the palates of its present patrons. Even this kind of entertainment had soon to give way to the performing elephant and the funambulist. The theatrical career of the old building finished when the

CONTINUATION AND DECADENCE

curtain fell on a piece called *False Evidence*, on Wednesday night, November 16th, 1892.

The new stage occupies the same spot as the old one, and may claim continuity with that which the Siddons trod. Not always, perhaps, was the art exhibited upon it of the highest; the web of its story, as Shakespeare says of that of our own lives, is of a mingled yarn, good and ill together. But—and this must be my excuse for trying to gather up some threads of it—here, on this spot, was for Wakefield, during all these years, "the glass in which, in every age and climate, human life has seen itself reflected, and has delighted, beyond all other pleasures, in pitying its own sorrows, in learning its own story, in watching its own fantastic developments, in foreshadowing its own fate, in smiling sadly for an hour over the still more fleeting representation of its own fleeting joys."

LIST OF SUBSCRIBERS.

Anderson, R. G. L., York Street
Ash, Alfred, Heathfield, Sandal
Atkinson, C. M., *M.A.*, Town Hall, Leeds

Banfield, A. E., Opera House, Westgate
Barratt, Percival, Bond Street (2 copies)
Barrett, Wilson, Grand Theatre, Leeds
Beaumont, Herbert, Hatfeild House
Benington, Henry, Wentworth Terrace
Beverley, James, *B.A.*, South Parade
Billington, John, 34, Burghley Road, London, N.W.
Bolland, A. P., Carter Street
Bolton, Major, Wentworth Terrace
Brear, Haydn, Northgate
Bruce, Samuel, *LL.B.*, *J.P.*, St. John's House
Bullock, Rev. R. G. P., *M.A.*, St. Martin's Vicarage, Leeds
Burkinshaw, W. H., Victoria Cottage, Balne Lane

Cater, James, 17, Marlboro' Road, Bradford
Chadwick, William, 8, Lansdowne Terrace
Chalmers, Rev. A., St. John's, (2 copies)
Chapman, Herbert, West Riding Bank

LIST OF SUBSCRIBERS.

Charlesworth, John, King Street
Childe, H. S., St. John's Villa
Claridge, W., *M.A.*, Market Street, Bradford
Clarkson, Miss, Alverthorpe Hall
Clarkson, Henry, Alverthorpe Hall
Curties, Rev. T. Arthur, *M.A.*, St. Michael's Vicarage

Dickons, J. N., 12, Oak Villas, Manningham
Dixon, W. Vibart, St. John's
Dove, John, Westgate Common

Eastwood, Andrew, Ash Road, Headingley
Eastwood, Frank, Ash Road, Headingley
Ellerton, G. V., St. John's

Farrah, John, Low Harrogate
Federer, Charles A., *L.C.P.*, 8, Hallfield Road, Bradford
Fennell, Charles W., Wood Street
Fennell, Richard, 4, Westfield Park
Fennell, Walter, Snow Hill View
Fernandes, G. W. L., Ackworth House, Pontefract
Fernandes, J. L., Tavora House, Grange-over-Sands

Galloway, F. C., Greenfield House, West Bowling, Bradford.
Gentlemen's Book Club, The (R. E. Langhorne)

LIST OF SUBSCRIBERS.

Glossop, Wm., Beckett's Bank Chambers, Bradford
Glover, B. F., Wood Street
Goldsbrough, G. H., Field Head, Stanley
Gould, G. D., St. John's
Graham, C. E., Registry Cottage
Greaves, J. O., *J.P.*, St. John's
Green, Captain H. G. E., St. John's

Haigh, Miss, Ivy Cottage, Stanley
Haigh, Jonathan, St. John's (2 copies)
Hainsworth, Lewis, 44, Tyrrel Street, Bradford
Haldane, G. W., Sandal
Hall, John, 9, Westgate
Haworth, F. Ernest, Stanley Grange
Hesling, John, Rydal Mount, Leeds Road
Hick, Matthew B., St. John's (3 copies)
Holmes, George, Harthill, Sheffield
Horne, W. F. L., *B.A.*, Sandal
Hughes, W. H., 33, Park Lane
Hurst, Mrs., Crofton Old Hall

Jaggar, Joseph, 17, Bradford Road

Kingswell, W. H., Northgate
Knight, Miss, 8, Lansdowne Terrace

LIST OF SUBSCRIBERS.

Langhorne, R. E., Woolley Moor House, Chapelthorpe
Leatham, Claude, Wentbridge, Pontefract
Lee, Fred, Northgate
Lee, J. H., 15, St. John's Square
Lewis, Mrs. Bevan, West Riding Asylum

Manton, John N., *L.D.S.*, *R.S.C.*,*Eng.*, South Parade
Marks, W. W., Shire Hall, Bedford
Marriott, W. T., *J.P.*, Sandal Grange (2 copies)
Masterman, George, King Street
Merry, M. F., 14, St. John's Square
Mortimer, Charles, Milwaukee, Wisconsin, U.S.A.

Northorpe, W. L., St. John's
Norwood, Captain W., Snow Hill View

Oxley, Miss Frances E., Bond Street

Parkinson, Mrs., Springfield Place, Barnsley
Peacock, Matthew H., *M.A.*, *Mus. Bac.*, Grammar School
Perkin, F. K., Northgate
Pickard, W., West Riding Registry of Deeds
Pickering, T. W., Attleborough, Nuneaton
Plews, H., St. John's Square
Poppleton, Richard, Stonecliffe, Horbury
Preston, T. L. C., 6, Eastmoor Road

LIST OF SUBSCRIBERS.

Radford, Geo. H., *LL.B.*, 40, Chancery Lane, London
Roberts, C. C., Snow Hill Lodge
Roberts, George, Lofthouse
Roche, G. B., The Towers, Bond Street

Scott, John, Sandal
Senior, Mrs., Bond Street
Sherwood, B., Opera House, Westgate
Simpson, Fred, Westfield Grove
Simpson, J. F., 211, Kirkgate
Skidmore, Charles, Bradford (2 copies)
Smith, A. D., Stoneleigh, Stanley
Statter, W. A., Thornhill House
Swire, John, Westfield Grove

Taylor, Major, *J.P.*, The Towers, Bond Street
Tomlinson, W. H. B., *J.P.*, Cliffe Tree House
Townend, W., Oakenshaw (2 copies)

Wadsworth, Mrs., Belgravia Towers, St. John's
Walker, H. Secker, Park Square, Leeds
Walker, Thomas, *J.P.*, Oakwood Grange, Roundhay, Leeds
Walker, J. W., *F.S.A.*, The Elms, Bond Street
Watson, William, The Gables, St. John's
West, Stephen H., *M.A.*, Hatfeild Hall, Stanley

LIST OF SUBSCRIBERS.

White, J. Fletcher, St. John's
Whitelegge, B. A., *M.D.*, St. John's
Whiteley, B., *F.I.J.*, Caxton House
Winter, William, Poulton Road, Southport
Wood, Butler, Free Library, Bradford
Wright, T. G., *M.D.*, Northgate

www.ingramcontent.com/pod-product-compliance
Lightning Source LLC
Chambersburg PA
CBHW030341170426
43202CB00010B/1196